Love Colour

Anna Starmer

Love Colour

Choosing colours to live with

IVY PRESS

First published in the UK in 2018 by
Ivy Press
An imprint of The Quarto Group
The Old Brewery, 6 Blundell Street
London N7 9BH, United Kingdom
T (0)20 7700 6700 F (0)20 7700 8066
www.QuartoKnows.com

British Library Cataloguing-in-Publication Data
A catalogue record for this book is available from
the British Library

ISBN: 978-1-78240-578-8

This book was conceived, designed, and produced by
Ivy Press
58 West Street, Brighton BN1 2RA, United Kingdom

Publisher Susan Kelly
Project Editor Stephanie Evans
Design Studio Noel
Editorial Assistant Niamh Jones

Cover image: Anna Starmer (wall paint Mid Azure Green (96): Little Greene
Paint Company; 'Blair' cushions: Christina Lundsteen)

Printed in China

10 9 8 7 6 5 4 3

CONTENTS

—

INTRODUCTION

Colour is a powerful, emotive subject. Everyone has an opinion on colour, and the range of colour choices on offer today is vast and can be complicated. For as long as I can remember, I have been rather obsessed by colour, collecting, photographing, painting, dyeing and telling stories with colours. Choosing colours, for me, is a personal expression, affected by a deep-rooted emotion or feeling. I am, of course, influenced by the world around me, by design trends and nature's seasons, by changing attitudes and tastes. I love to people-watch, and to study how our lifestyles and the choices we make affect the colours we desire in our lives. Colour is transformative and our tastes may shift with time; we can evolve and build our colour ideas to suit our changing lives and our current obsessions.

The colours we choose are ultimately a statement about who we are, what we love, and how we want to live.

From the clothes we wear to the colour of our front door, the colour decisions we all make often come from an immediate response, a very personal connection to certain colours. In my career, I have spent many years collaborating with clients to decipher the infinite rainbow in front of them, and to help them choose colours that are perfect for their product or style. In writing this book I hope to lead you through the potentially overwhelming abundance of colour choices and back to your true self, to the colours that you love the most.

Be clear and honest about which colours you love and want to surround yourself with; these are the colours that resonate with you – they make you feel happy, calm and comfortable. Build confidence in your own colour style and identify your own personal, perfect shades. Remember that your home is for you, there is no right or wrong way with colour – simply trust your own instincts.

Left: In the studio, collections of objects and photography inspire new colour creations for both fashion and interior design ideas.

Right: The musings of a colour consultant: dyed threads, material samples, paint swatches and photographs all come together to inspire alluring colour combinations and new ideas for surface and design.

Of all the elements that, as decorators and homemakers, we can add to our personal environments, colour is one of the most dynamic and cost-effective ways to transform a space. Colour has instant impact and elicits a strong and personal response. It works on a subconscious level – we instinctively know whether we like or dislike a colour scheme. By surrounding ourselves with the right colours we can enhance our emotional well being and improve our day-to-day mood.

A dwelling only truly becomes a home when it is filled with life: family, friends, animals and plants. Collectables and personal keepsakes speak of our private history, they thread stories and memories through our home. Treasures collected on our travels, books, ornaments, and cherished artworks all weave together to create our own personal colour palette. So many of our design decisions are built around the way we live and the necessities of our daily routines. The specific function and purpose of each room drives the ways in which we inhabit it; colour can be used to enhance these spaces, helping each room feel more defined and purposeful. The ways in which colours affect and alter one another can seem a touch of magic; light and surface too can transform the ways we see a colour.

There are no rules when decorating your home; your space is your blank canvas upon which to play with colour and pattern. Get up close and personal with your colours; experiment with bright colour flashes and accents, notice the way subtle nuances or tones can blur and blend to create a perfect room scheme.

Love Colour is an adventure in colour, a treasure box of ideas and inspiration gathered from around the world suggesting timeless, beautiful colour solutions for your home.

Love colour, it will fill your home with love, life, laughter and light.

Anna Starmer

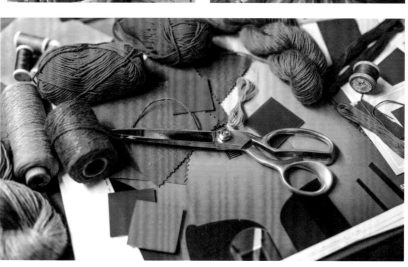

FINDING INSPIRATION

———

Colour inspiration is all around you; it's just knowing where to look for it and how to record it. In today's world most of us are afforded the luxury of having a camera in our handbag or pocket. Photograph things that appeal to you. The particular grey of an old stone wall might catch your eye, or you might gravitate towards a lampshade you spy in a restaurant, or you might simply love the colours in your best friend's kitchen.

So make a habit of collecting images. Save pages from magazines or print off photographs that you come across online. Collate and store your images in files or create mood boards. Why not record things in a scrapbook? Try grouping similarly coloured images together and you will start to understand how these work with one another. Consider also the surface textures, materials and patterns that feature in the images. What appeals to you? Perhaps you want to go all out and embrace pattern clashing, or you may want something more subtle. Unless you mix and match images together you won't know what engages you.

Collecting colour samples and creating your own mood boards in this way will help you to define your own style and confirm which colours are suited to you and your lifestyle. Most of us do not live in show homes. Our homes are for living in, which is why you want to ensure the colour schemes you choose reflect your own taste and ideas. Be influenced and inspired by interiors magazines and online mood board or pinning sites, but be careful not to be dazzled by fashion into following a scheme or a trend that is just not suited to your space or way of life. Colour combinations go in and out of fashion, and chances are that you will quickly fall out of love with a scheme that you have simply copied from the pages of a glossy magazine.

GATHERING TREASURE

Choosing the best colours for you and your interior scheme can be a difficult task, given the seemingly endless array of ideas and inspiration available. It is important to recognize and acknowledge your own favourite colours and styles, and hold on to your vision, even when you are bombarded with paint shade cards, fabric swatches, style guides and other people's opinions. Follow a few basic steps to boost your colour confidence and help simplify the task ahead.

The golden rule in decorating is that if you really love something, you will enjoy living with it for many years. Trust your instincts: your home is your own space, and you should fill it with what pleases you.

Begin by noticing the detail and colours that shape our environment and you'll quickly discover that you are drawn to things principally because of their colour. Once you identify which colours truly make your heart sing, you can start to bring objects together to create an easily accessible visual record. You get an immediate sense of surface finish and texture from handling physical objects rather than simply looking at images in print or on a screen. Keep everything that catches your eye, a shiny sweet wrapper, a favourite nail polish, an old faded button, a washed pebble or an iridescent feather; they can all provide inspiration for that perfect shade.

Your personal collection of treasures is the starting point for your colour journey. By gathering together items that you have an emotional attachment to, and igniting your inner passion for colour, you will become more confident about using the colours you love to decorate your home.

Left and right: Collate and assemble your found treasures together, from paint swatches and fabric samples to objects that resonate with you. Note how surface and material plays with colour, and play with different shades against one another to see which you love the most. .

DEFINE YOUR OWN STYLE

We each see colour in our own unique and personal way, and we are all affected by colour differently. However, many of us struggle to identify our own style when it comes to decorating our homes. It is so easy to be overwhelmed by choice and decorating a home is such a big investment that we don't want to get it wrong. Whether you have just moved into your first apartment, or you feel you need to stamp more of your own style on an existing space, with a little planning you can curate a room that ticks all the right boxes – for you!

Spending time in each space before you make decorating decisions is so important. Look closely at existing objects, features and the details within a room. Have you tried to create a style before, or do you simply have a collection of furniture that has been accumulated over the last ten years? Is there something in this room that you absolutely cannot live without – a favourite painting, a handmade cushion, a box of shells collected on holiday? Have a good clear out before you start to decorate. Edit and minimize your belongings. Decluttering your space will help to give you a clearer vision of your own ideas. Only keep objects, art, furniture and accessories that you love, or that you need.

Now you can begin to layer on new colour and texture. Referring to your mood boards and your collection of treasures, start to define colours for your scheme. Order fabric swatches or paint samples and start to play with colour on surfaces and materials. Inspect the colours in your wardrobe too – often these directly reflect your favourite palette and hues. Continue to look at your colours together, and spot how one colour is affected by another. Take your curated treasures with you to the paint store and match their colours directly with the paint charts. Become a colour geek!

Right: It's easy to get into the habit of grouping together objects in textures and colours that appeal to you. Placing objects together is one way to develop confidence when selecting colours for your decorating scheme.

CHOOSING COLOUR

Collected images and physical objects create not only a visual impression of a colour, but also a tactility, a surface or a feeling we associate with that colour. Often our colour inspirations are material inspirations as well; consider the surfaces and textures of your objects, and the materials they are made from. Have you collected swatches of matt, natural linen and greyed, chalky pebbles to inspire softened, subtle colours from nature? Or perhaps your inner magpie is drawn to shiny, glossy treasure, coloured glass, sequin fabrics and mirrored finishes in striking shades of indigo and sapphire.

Another key step before you commit to a scheme is to appraise the colours you are drawn to within the space you are looking to transform. Assess the shape and the function of the room, and consider any furniture that is staying. Look at colour in different areas of the room, next to the window, or closer to the floor – and watch how colours can appear stronger or softer at different times of the day. Colours are deeply affected by light and shade, as well as by the other colours which surround them.

Lay out your treasures on a table or on the floor, and gauge which items work best together. Perhaps the soft green of a fern leaf is just the perfect cool shade next to a vintage velvet lavender purse? Look for harmony both in colour combinations and surfaces. Play with your mood objects until you find combinations that just feel right. Remember the golden rule for making decisions about colour: if you instinctively love something, you will enjoy living with it for many years to come.

Left: An array of rich blues comes to life through opposing surfaces and materials. Notice the way a glossy metallic finish lifts and shines light into an ocean blue, or how densely dyed felted wool absorbs and adds shadow to inky indigo. Layering contrasting tones of the same colour on different surfaces throughout a single scheme is a very effective technique.

MOOD & EMOTION

Choosing the right colours to suit you and your emotional well being can have a positive effect on the way you feel and the way you live at home. It has been proven that colours really do affect the mood of a space, and every colour ignites a unique and emotional response in the viewer. Colours influence and interact with our emotional and spiritual well being, heighten the senses and help to restore the balance between mind and body. There are some simple, recognized connections between colour and emotion, blues and greens are said to connect us to nature and so feel calming; bright sunshine yellow boosts energy levels and lifts our moods, making it a perfect choice for kitchens.

This concept goes well beyond the basic notions of colour and mood. Here we are analysing how you want to feel in your home because each of us individually sees and tunes into colour in our own unique way. To some, a pure white scheme will feel instantly serene and restful; yet to others, the same scheme may feel cold and unnatural or unhomely.

It is vital that your scheme not only looks good, but also tunes into your own sensual needs. Your home needs to feel warm and inviting. We are highly intuitive and all of the senses can be put to use when we are designing an interior. Consider how the surfaces need to feel in order to create a dark and cosy living room; think of the perfect scented candle in the bedroom and how its soft

flickering light might enhance the delicate colour on the walls; or how the serenity of a garden room is enhanced when the walls are painted in palest smoke grey.

Mood and atmosphere, like colour, are affected by light. Simply switching off bright overhead lights and lighting a few candles instead can transform a space. Really consider your room and the ambience you would like to create, dream of how you long to feel when the room is complete, and write down the words that spring to mind, such as calm and reflective, or happy and sociable. Assess these words and moods in colour terms – which colour makes you feel calm, is it blue or lavender, pure white or soft pale peach? Happy colours are often bold and bright – think of yellow or orange – but for some rooms, a clear cool aqua blue may evoke just the right upbeat, energetic mood that you require.

Bringing an emotional aspect to your colour designs in turn connects you to the world you live in. It reminds us that we are sentient beings, and that we need to live, love, laugh and cry. We need spaces in which to sleep and be restful, spaces in which to socialize or play loud music, spaces in which to think and work. Using the right colours can help us to connect with the human tasks we need to do at home, and to the emotional needs elicited throughout life. If you design with your emotional needs up front, you will instinctively bring intimacy and personality into your home.

CALM & PALE

By introducing calming colours and soft textures into our living spaces, we can completely alter the ambience in our homes; a bedroom becomes a comforting haven full of deep sleep and good dreams; the bathroom is transformed from a simple place to wash to your very own at-home wellness spa.

For a colour scheme to be calming it needs to be easy on the eye and the senses. Choose colours that are soft and with a similar tone, or layer subtle nuances of light and dark versions of the same shade. Avoid harsh contrast or patterns containing clashing colours. Dusted, smudged or chalky colours have a soft quality about them. They simply merge into the surroundings and melt away our stress. Pale, indistinct colours, such as pearly grey, milky white or vanilla cream, have a soft, radiant quality and reflect light back into a room, naturally lifting the spirits. Colours connected to the whites feel clear and uncluttered. These neutral tints act as emotional cleansing, helping to ease our busy minds. Calm colours are like new beginnings, filled with promise and a sense of optimism.

Far left: The palest of shades are enhanced and softened through textured surfaces. Powdery clay-coloured painted walls and naturally crumpled linens alleviate any coolness in the colours and subdue this harmonious colour palette.

Above and left: Layers of palest grey and off-whites reflect and absorb the light, evoking an aura of tranquillity, an almost spiritual stillness.

DARK & SATURATED

It is a misconception that decorating with dark colours can make a space look small and gloomy. Nothing could be further from the truth. Clever use of dark colours can create a bold and striking space filled with drama. Take inspiration from the interiors of gentlemen's clubs, underground secret dining dens and lavish Victorian ladies' salons. These rich and often decadent spaces were filled with opulent materials, dark wood panelling, and low theatrical lighting.

A dining room, cosy lounge or a poorly lit entrance hall is the ideal canvas for a saturated colour scheme. Be bold and create a design that has impact. Dark inky shades of midnight blue or charcoal create the illusion of walls receding, thus making a space appear bigger than it is. If a room is starved of natural light, painting it white will only make it feel colder. Rich and saturated colours create warmth, so use these with confidence. Fill your space with surfaces that can absorb and reflect light, to enhance the depth of the colour. Glossy lacquered tabletops, tinted mirrors or richly coloured glass will all bounce light around the room. Consider textures and fabrics too. Introduce jewel-coloured velvets and silks. Play with brighter and lighter colours against your deep backgrounds and watch how shades come to life when enveloped in darkness.

Above and right: Deep navy or inky blue acts as the perfect ground colour on which to layer your highlights and accents. Candy-pink fabrics and a floor-to-ceiling display of antique books are given an air of instant sophistication and glamour when defined by darkness.

Far right: Black is an unexpected choice for a bedroom, but here the delicate hand-drawn graphic wallpaper and metallic gold surfaces bring warmth and light, creating a luminous, not gloomy, atmosphere.

BRIGHT POPS OF COLOUR

Bright colours can be like a blast of vitality, a vitamin boost to the senses. Bright yellow is akin to sunshine and can literally make us feel happy. Oranges and pinks are the get-up-and-go colours that motivate and enhance the spirit.

However, bright colours may not be ideal for every room in your home. A bedroom, for example, generally needs to be calm and restful. Often it is more pleasing on the eye to use bright colours in clever bursts or 'pops'. A gorgeous hot shade of magenta or vibrant marmalade orange really comes alive when set against a pale grey background. Red and green are complementary colours and work fantastically together, as do blue and orange. An overload of colour and pattern can be effective, but keep this to a single area within an otherwise simple room scheme.

Pattern and print offer the perfect way to add a flash of bright colour. Choose fun cushions with neon trims for a sofa, or vibrant colourful artworks to hang in a child's bedroom. Bright colour does not have to dominate your scheme. Use it in accessories, textiles and details to introduce irreverence without overloading the senses.

Increasingly, our homes need to be multifunctional. By focusing the use of high-octane contrasting colours you can create zones within the home and visually define the different functions of a room.

Consider the use of contrasting colours from one room to another. Bright, welcoming colour in an entrance hall will lead the visitor through to a cool interior beyond. Play with clashing colours and see the effect of juxtaposing cool and warm colours.

Left: Modern dye processes and technology in mixing colours afford us a vast array of choice when searching for the perfect colour. It is fun to be inspired by the rainbow of colours on offer, but avoid getting overloaded or confused by the amount of choice in front of you.

Above: Contrasting colours from room to room define the entrance from the interior of this open-plan home in India. Light and shadow further accentuate the different atmospheres created by the colours.

WARM COLOURS

A home needs to be comfortable and nurturing. Warm colours are inviting and have the power to envelop us. Shades of red, orange and yellow, the colours of fire, have natural associations of warmth. Golden ripened wheat, sun-kissed sand dunes, and cosy lamb's wool are all-embracing colours that will fill a room with warmth and light. Spicy, hot colours such as mango chutney, paprika red and cinnamon are great if you want to create a warm and inviting scheme.

Apply glowing colours to areas in your home that lack natural light. A cold and uninviting entrance hall or stairwell is immediately transformed through the addition of mimosa yellow walls. A dark and characterless downstairs bathroom becomes a welcoming retreat when daubed from top to bottom in the rich and succulent colour of olive oil.

Think about surfaces and materials that will enhance and exaggerate this sense of warmth; natural sandstone and red brick do this well. Introduce plump cushions, deep-pile rugs and throws to wrap up in when the temperature drops. Lighting can make or break a design scheme so choose it carefully. Avoid harsh, bright overhead artificial lighting as this can make a room feel instantly cold. Soft ambient lighting will add to a feeling of warmth in any room. Candlelight and an open fire give instant heat to any setting, indoors or outside, and can make a space feel immediately more intimate and welcoming.

Above: Low light adds warmth and these patterned lanterns provide a pleasing red glow that will soften any interior scheme.

Right: A sun-filled patio is enhanced by the addition of bright orange textiles. They provide a shot of hot colour to this balmy outdoor corner.

Far right: Imagine immersing yourself in a bathroom painted entirely the colour of olive oil. This luxuriously decadent shade is as deep, rich and alluring as pure gold.

COOL COLOURS

——

You might ask why would you want to create a colour scheme that features cool colours. Surely our homes need to be filled with warmth, light and an inviting atmosphere? Yet there are spaces in which cool shades really do work their magic. Cool colours can feel as fresh as the morning dew on the grass, or subdued and blurred, like mist in autumn. It is said that cool blues can reduce blood pressure and slow the heart rate and, as such, cool colours are perfect calming shades for a bedroom or bathroom. Just remember to layer up snug and welcoming fabrics and textures to prevent the space from feeling cold.

Cool colours are intrinsically linked to the natural world: picture cool watery blues and refreshing spring greens. Although cool colours are typically blue, green and violet, we can also add to these cooler shades of greys and off-whites, even cooler blueish tints of pink.

Cool colours can have dramatically different effects depending on the climate and weather patterns. Cool colours are heightened or changed depending on the natural light in a room. Spaces that do not receive generous amounts of warm sunlight may not fare well if filled with cooling colours.

It is definitely a good idea to buy paint tester pots and cover large sheets of paper with your selected choices. Select colours wisely because ones that look good on a tiny swatch may seem very cold when covering an entire wall. Attach the painted sheets to the walls and live with these for a couple of weeks to determine how you truly feel about a colour scheme. Opt for shades with a 'warmer' tint, say summer sky blues. If you are decorating with a grey-based colour scheme, avoid greys with blueish undertones. Instead, choose greys such as smoke, dove or feather, all of which have a warmer hue, and a pinkish, natural tint.

Left: Layers of greenish tinted blues are blended together through paint and textiles to create a softened and cosy bedroom that still feels elegant and tranquil.

Above: Cool shades of grey and dusky blues are enlivened by afternoon sun streaming through the windows. A roaring fire and heavy, textural bedding combine to make this a warm, seductive bedroom, despite the cool colour palette.

HUE & TONE

In colour terms, hue and tone usually relate to colours within a similar colour family or group. Hue refers to the pure pigment of a colour. The primary colours are red, blue and yellow – and all colours have a relation to these three primary shades. For instance, a deep ocean-coloured blanket could have a blue hue and a golden-painted wall could have a yellow hue.

Mixing colours together with grey, or tinting and shading a colour, creates what is referred to as a tone of colour. A tint is a colour that has been mixed with white, increasing lightness, and a shade is one that

has been mixed with black, reducing lightness. Play around with tone, lightness and depth of colour within a room scheme. It can be very effective to choose a colour scheme that is derived from a single hue. Choose a base colour such as olive green, and then layer on top varying greens like herb, avocado and khaki, making sure to stay close to the yellowish tints of the original olive colour.

Above and right: Nature offers up an unending array of green hues and tones. Play with the effects of using these colours together for a pleasing, considered design statement.

CONTRAST COLOUR

Contrast can be introduced into a scheme in a variety of ways, the most obvious being through the use of contrasting colours. One way of implementing this would be to select colours at the extreme ends of light and dark – white and black being the most obvious example. However, a soft nude and a dark sage green, would also work beautifully. Another way to achieve contrast is by taking colours that oppose one another on the colour spectrum. This means mixing the cool colours, blue, green and violet, with the warmer colour families of red, orange and yellow. A deep indigo blue-painted living room with a bright ochre yellow velvet sofa would be a perfect example of colour contrast. Cleverly juxtaposed cool and warm colours can create an incredibly powerful colour palette.

Whether you choose a bold hot pink against a dark inky background, or a softer cool sky blue and a warm, peachy desert sand colour, the correct balance of colour is key. A flash of bright colour in the corner of a dark room will lift that space and draw the eye to it. As in any well-designed space, it is important that one colour takes the dominant role and the other becomes the accent shade, used in furniture, textiles and accessories.

Contrast can be introduced through pattern too. Don't forget about the importance of wallpaper and window dressing. And, of course, contrast is not just about colour; different textures and surfaces add depth and warmth to your interior scheme.

Left: The opposing shades of sky blue and warm, peachy terracotta complement one another in this cityscape of Jodhpur in India.

Above and right: Dark charcoal and nearly black shades create a dramatic backdrop upon which to play with contrasting colours and textures. Choose graphic monochrome juxtapositions throughout your scheme, or add a flash of unexpected hot pink.

TEXTURE & SURFACE

Colour and pattern can definitely add to our sense of well being and relaxation at home, but how things feel to touch is just as important. Humans naturally respond to touch and when we touch something super soft or beautifully smooth it makes us feel good. Textures and surface finishes should not be skimped over. Pay them as much attention as you would colour when devising a room scheme. The structure of any material will have an absolute effect on the colours you wish to use. Consider how glossy, light-reflective materials lift, enhance and exaggerate any colour applied, perfect for high-contrast opposing schemes with dark and light colours mixed. Shiny resin, polished ceramic glaze and mirrored effects will also create a different mood in the room, a more dramatic and contrasting palette is defined, because colours are refracted and enlightened by these surfaces.

In contrast, fluffy textiles, natural skins, suede, velvet and matt painterly finishes absorb the light, and they can flatten and dull the chosen colours. Brushed, blurred and textural finishes give colours a softened, hazy aura, and a more genteel or quiet finish. There are less harsh contrasts or clashes, as colours merge and blend across softened materials, lending themselves perfectly to tonal schemes and greyed-off mid-toned colours.

Left: A stack of vintage fabrics shows the effect of texture on a rich array of colours. Glossy, golden tassels shimmer and shine, rich lustrous velvets let the light in and colours seem to glow.

Above: Matt, unpolished surfaces absorb and affect colour in an alluring way. The imperfections in clay pots and natural woven linen textures give an undulating finish which is never flat – and often you can see many colours, not just one.

Right: A cherished collection of antique Christmas baubles twinkle and sparkle under the lights. The shiny painted glass surface illuminates the fun candy pinks and emerald greens.

PATTERN & PRINT

—

Is there a room in your home that is looking a little tired or unloved? It is simple to inject some life and personality into it by introducing pattern. Pattern can be used in many different ways, from flooring to upholstery, lampshades to curtains and blinds, tiling, wallpaper, accessories, tableware, textiles and throws. Be as bold or as subtle as you like. Keep colour combinations simple and make your pattern the focus of the room or mix and match patterns together – just always ensure you are combining patterns that have the same colour palette, for example blue and white stripes layered together with a blue floral motif.

Consider the space you want to transform and how pattern could be used. You could accentuate an architectural feature, say a chimney breast, or a dark corner, with a bold wallpaper. Perhaps use pattern on the floor and keep all other surfaces plain. Pick out a single contrast colour from your pattern as a solid paint colour to smarten the finish.

Left and above: Scandinavian-inspired motifs are a naive take on decoration, great for a child's bedroom. Graphic wallpaper can introduce colour and humour to a scheme.

Right: A patchwork of encaustic tiles from Morocco brings a splash of unexpected warmth and colour to a cool farmhouse kitchen in Yorkshire, UK.

LIGHT & COLOUR

There is a natural daily cycle of light and dark, day and night known as the circadian rhythm. Our bodies, minds and spirits need both day and night in equal measures in order to thrive and survive. Lighting in our homes needs to function on a variety of levels to support and nurture us.

There are four main types of lighting in home interiors: natural daylight, task lighting, accent lighting and ambient lighting. Maximize the daylight in your homes wherever possible. Keep windows clear and use light-reflecting surfaces in rooms that may not have enough natural daylight.

Task lighting needs to be clear and bright, and focused on the areas in which specific jobs will be carried out, whether it's working at a computer, reading, sewing or cooking. For example, a kitchen will usually benefit from carefully considered task lighting, but you could soften the effect by having a low pendant light, fitted with a dimmer switch, over a kitchen table.

Accent lighting can add depth and shadow by focusing on specific objects or areas of a room. You may want to light up a corner of a room with a decorative patterned lamp, or spotlight a cherished painting or collection of ornaments as the centrepiece of your room scheme.

Finally ambient lighting is how you create mood. Ideally it should be warm and soft, gentle and diffused, to provide a relaxed atmosphere in which to unwind. It can come from wall or table lamps fitted with low-wattage bulbs, but the most evocative ambient light is that from a fire or candles, which cast a perfect warm light and exude a sense of well being.

Far left: Indistinct or darkened colours are immediately brought to life with the addition of light. Be aware that the yellowish glow of some lightbulbs affects and plays tricks with the way you see colours in a room.

Left and above: Make the most of the magic golden hour – that time between afternoon and evening as the sun sets. If you are lucky enough to have a space in your home that captures those last golden rays of light be sure to make it a focal point.

ARCHITECTURAL FEATURES

Whether you live in a modern apartment with clean lines and minimalist, open-plan rooms, a narrow townhouse, a low-ceilinged cottage or a converted warehouse, the shape and structure of your home will have an impact on the scheme you decide upon. Often a space has existing shapes or features that will need to be taken into consideration, such as a large chimney breast, a dark polished wooden floor, a sloping attic ceiling, or an oversized window frame. Work with and celebrate the idiosyncrasies of your home. Use colour, pattern, light and texture to enhance and accentuate key areas in a room. Take note of architectural features, such as

exposed brick or beams, and refer to their shade when selecting colours to use in close proximity. Contrast pale and bright colours from one room to another, adopt flashes of colour that draw the eye through your home.

Above: A well-designed and refined colour scheme of natural and neutral shades is used throughout this home. It is welcome, and unexpected, to catch a glimpse of the bright blue colour used in the family room.

Right: An oversized decorative lampshade draws the eye up into a double-height ceiling. This bright and welcoming space embraces natural wooden beams and stone walls and uses colours that allow the natural materials to sing out.

HOW TO USE THIS BOOK

Love Colour equips you with the creative knowledge you need before you begin to decorate your home. It is dedicated to helping you to decipher colour and to make lasting choices that are right for you and your space. Its aim is to encourage you to build your own colour confidence, trust your own tastes and instincts, and to inspire you to create successful schemes before you make crucial decisions at a paint supplier's or in a fabrics and furnishings store. The interior photography and inspirational images present unique and considered approaches to colour. At a glance, you will see how colour affects other colours and why certain combinations are so effective, and the text identifies contrasting or complementary shades, so that you understand how colour really works.

The book is organized by colour theme. Every page offers exciting applications of colour, from bright and bold to pale and soothing. You may be instantly drawn to your favourite group of colours, or spot an unexpected combination, which is perfect for your current project. Each chapter has images and colours across the range, from light to dark: for example, from sky to indigo blue, proposing new ideas and nuances of blues throughout. The Natural chapter offers a gentle collection of colours, inspired by simple, unprocessed materials and finishes such as wood, clay, stone and wicker.

When working with colour never underestimate the importance of surface, texture, light and shade. These elements profoundly shift and transform the appearance of colours. The text makes detailed reference to the effect of different materials and finishes, and the photographs show you how light is absorbed or reflected by different surfaces, and the way that colours respond to the surface to which they are applied, becoming deep and indulgent, or light and whitened.

Alongside the photographs are colour bars that pick out the key palette ideas, showing you the most beautiful and inspirational ways to use colour. These simple panels are a snapshot of the proportions of colours that make a scheme successful. The example on the opposite page explains how the colour bars work. A deep expanse of saturated blue dominates this room; this is the 'ground'

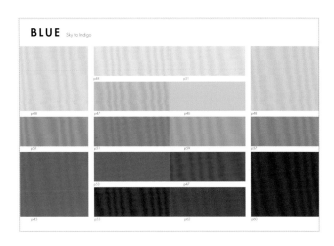

BLUE Sky to Indigo

colour. Notice how the blue shade makes up two-thirds of the overall colour bar. It is complemented by the warm brown tones of the polished floorboards and the white painted woodwork. These colours are shown in smaller blocks, denoting secondary or complementary shades. A flash of coral is used to contrasting effect on two vintage armchairs. It is the smallest block of colour here and yet possibly the most important. This highlight or accent shade of coral lifts the entire scheme and creates an original and well-considered design finish.

You can, of course, simply take these ideas and apply them to your own environment. If you love the look of a particular colour palette then use these colours in your own home. Take note of the proportion or 'weight' of each colour in the scheme, and consider the way that any one colour lifts and heightens the others.

In the back of the book is a handy pull-out booklet that contains swatches of key colours from every chapter. Use it to source your favourite colours when considering paint, fabrics or furniture. Take it with you to a paint store or an upholsterer's – the range of colours on offer today ensures your supplier will be able to provide a close match to any given shade.

Inspiring and achievable, *Love Colour* gives you the confidence to take risks, follow your heart and know that the results will be sensational.

ground

accent

accent

contrast

complementary

Above left: Swatches in the pull-out booklet are the shades from the book that are likely to feature prominently in your own schemes and palettes. These are the most usable colours, ones that may work throughout your home. Each page groups colours with a similar hue together (for instance, in blues are green-tinted blues and ones that are more red-tinted), helping you to understand which shades work best with one another.

Above: This deep dark greenish-blue is a wonderful ground on which to add pops and accents of colour. The cool blue is lifted and warmed by the bright coral-pink velvet upholstery. Glossy rich brown floorboards add a polished sheen, further lifting and enhancing the colours in the room. A clean white border formed by the skirting boards and woodwork finishes everything perfectly.

*"Let me die from having being drunk
on indigo skies, my liver… overflowing
with stars."* Sanober Khan

SKY TO INDIGO

BLUE

Positive and intense or calming and restorative, blue is the colour of both the
pinstripe suit and the denim shirt, of things nautical and naval; blue exudes
confidence, inspiration and familiarity. It marks our daylight hours, dawning
pale, becoming bright then drawing to a dark mysterious close. From cloudless
sky to delicate duck egg, piercing sapphire to ultramarine, the blues are
intrinsically linked with the natural world. These are energizing, refreshing
and invigorating colours in our homes.

As we are confronted daily with visual overload, it becomes ever more important that our private spaces are uncomplicated environments in which we can unwind and escape the stresses and strains of the outside world. Colour can be used in clever ways to help this quest for rest and relaxation, and the blues are perfect for invoking calm and balance.

Blues do not have to be cool, or make a room feel cold. Quite the opposite in fact. As the sun streams through the windows on a warm sunny day, blue tones can be the perfect colour choice to lift the spirits. Here, blues are used together with soft sandstone yellow and natural biscuit tints, creating a calm and balanced atmosphere of warmth with cool colour.

Use greenish blues and watery colours to create a restful space. The blue colour family has always been a favourite choice in the bathroom. Choose a mix of warmer and deeper tones of blue, reminiscent of the ocean, to prevent your bathroom from feeling too cold. A distressed paint finish on the walls can create warmth and natural cosiness in your space.

Left: Inspired by Ibiza's laid-back bohemian attitude, the summer sun picks out and reflects this greenish-blue, Mediterranean sea colour. Choose cooler shades of blue at the windows to help shade the room from the midday heat.

Above: Blues are an enduring choice for exterior and interior walls. Matt, weathered and aged or sunbleached surfaces play with the colours, reflecting light, absorbing and intensifying the blue shades. Experiment with mid-tone blues, from deep ocean greenish tones to the red-tinted or warmer, violet-hued blues.

Duck-egg blues inspire a beautiful palette of colours to play with, ranging from greenish tints through to clean, clear bluer tones. Soft green-blues act as a blank canvas, providing a perfect base on which to layer stronger colours and patterns and build up a unique scheme. Soft reds or dusted terracotta work well, as the cool and warm colours contrast and complement one another.

Above: These flat levels of blue act like neutral shades, just as a grey would, seamlessly blending into the surroundings. Accents of strong olive green and shades of spiced reds or rusted oranges breathe warmth into these schemes.

Right: Play around with traditional methods of decorating a room. Use your main colour on the ceiling and the woodwork, instead of the walls. Allow the natural patina and texture of bare plaster walls to remain untouched, celebrating the intricate detail and original colours of an exposed surface.

Left: Blue works well in so many colour combinations. Fresh summer sky blue is beautiful for exterior walls. Different shades and depths of blue can be perfect in many spaces at home. Use deep ancient indigo for dinner plates or table linen. Choose vibrant and revitalizing aqua and tropical turquoise in the bathroom in fun geometric floor tiles or stacks of textured patterned towels.

Right: The Medina of Fez, Morocco, is one of the largest and most ancient walled cities in the world. Nestled into the heart of this endless maze of narrow alleyways lined with local craftsmen, lies a natural oasis. This house, painted in shades of sky and bluebell, offers a fresh and vibrant welcome after the intense heat of the city.

Blue and white form a classic colour combination, both in the home and in our wardrobes. Evoking the seaside, deckchairs and coastal nautical stripes, this fresh and invigorating colour pairing will take you back to holidays and afternoons spent by the sea. Crystalline or mineral blues reflect the light. Play with colours from the sky, sea and sandy white beaches, look closely and note the different shades. Nothing here is simply blue, and nothing is actually white; pale sand, creamy whites and sun-kissed peachy whites all add warmth and soften the scheme. Tonal shades of blue merge effortlessly from indoors to outside. Try light and deep blues together in a single scheme, contrasting clear and pale shades with deep and intense. Where possible, use natural surfaces with a matt finish to enhance the depth of colour. Layers of blues range from turquoise to periwinkle, forget-me-not to deeper tropical ocean or jewel blues, through to darker accent shades of indigo.

Pattern and texture can elevate a palette of simple colours into something quite magical and extraordinary. No surface here is flat and the tactile imperfections of individually crafted features – from the faded plaster and relief detailing to the intricately carved and painted wood and hand-embroidered cloth – reveal the many shades of blue in these aged and decorated surfaces. Notice how well blues and oranges enhance one another.

Left and above: This unique shade of blue is mixed only in the city of Jodhpur in India, known as the Blue City, where it adorns most of the ancient walls and archways. A flash of bright orange sari fabric or a bright poppy red detail on a painted carved door breaks up the cooling blue shades.

Following pages: Deep and arresting colours jostle and vie for attention in this townhouse. The high ceilings and grand marble fireplace allow space for deep and intense colours to come to life. Pops and details in golden yellow and clever accent lighting lift the colours and enliven the entire theatrical scene.

Embrace opportunities to use pattern in unusual ways. Colour and decoration can lead visitors through your home, highlighting dark corners and bringing vibrancy to tired areas. Vivid turquoise or electric blue are bold colours to incorporate into a room scheme and they will add originality and character; you may not want to fill an entire room with such bright blues, but they work well as accent colours used in a thoughtful and precise design.

Left and above: A decorative patterned lampshade or a wallpapered alcove will add a point of focus to your room. An accent shade of deep plum on textiles is a perfect complementary shade within this blue scheme. Glossy, high-sheen fabrics reflect light and intensify the richness of the colour palette.

Design an interior around things you love, objects that are full of memories and sentimental value. Don't hide your keepsakes away. Display these collections as they can often add a pop of colour to your colour scheme. Layer accents of contrasting colours; white is clear and sharp, while soft oranges and natural wood colours add warmth to the blue background.

Deep inky blues have a rich and alluring history. These evocative colours are linked to ancient rituals and tribal traditions. The saturated blue tones are said to have a connection with the heavenly night sky and aid an awakening of the senses. Indigo and deep blues can elevate a room scheme, creating a space that is both tranquil and meditative, yet also invigorating and inspiring.

For centuries the colour indigo was rare and sought after in the West. This dark and mysterious plant dye, as exotic as spices and as valuable as gold, was traded through long-established merchant routes. From African Dogon tribal cloth to Japanese shibori fabrics, indigo is experiencing a revival, its natural quality and intense colour can add a luxurious depth when used in the home.

Left and above: Build layers of pattern and decoration on your blue surfaces. Simple, hand-painted or wood-blocked motifs can be applied to any surface. Paint a white floral motif on your front door, hang panels of Japanese-inspired papers on a feature wall, or seek out vintage indigo kimono fabric to fashion cushions for your living room.

Left: Use deep inky colour on both the walls and a shelving unit to create an invisible display case, where inspirational books and favourite objects can be grouped together in colour coordinated families.

Right: Extract different tones from your accent colours and feature them against a dark blue wall. Here, floral pinks are the inspiration; bougainvillea is a deep and vibrant magenta, apple blossom is pretty and pastel, rose pinks are usually mid-toned and dusty. Layer colour in soft furnishing fabrics such as wool or velvet. You could even choose a different shade of pink to cover each chair in a room.

Dark midnight skies and inky blue backdrops create the perfect canvas on which to play with brighter colours. Contrasting hot colours are perfect against this rich base, as coral reds and fragrant, floral pinks sing out against the deep and captivating blues. Shades that are not true primary colours work best, avoid true blue with bright red, it may appear too childish or naive. Deep blue and coral offer a more refined and sophisticated scheme – perfect for living or dining rooms.

Be confident with dark colours in small spaces. It is true that large rooms with high ceilings are made more intimate and inviting through the use of deep and seductive colours, but choose rich and captivating shades of ocean blue for stairwells and small entrance halls too, to create a sense of drama and unexpected delight. Dark colours actually make small spaces seem larger and you can be adventurous with lighting to create flamboyant and enchanting interior spaces.

Surface and texture can enhance a colour scheme dramatically. Introducing a high-gloss surface such as a table top into an otherwise matt and restrained scheme intensifies an accent pop of brighter colour. The reflective surface also bounces light around the room. Try adding contrasting textures within a room and see how colour and light are affected by the different materials.

Left and above: Notice that there is no primary blue in either of these schemes; use softened or darkened shades of blue when you feature bright poppy red or ruby accents. Use your accent colour wisely to create a sense of drama; focus on a single chair, or a central dining table, keeping the rest of the space cool and clear. Try to keep things simple when you work with contrasting colours.

"Green is the prime colour of the world,
and that from which its loveliness arises."

Pedro Calderón de la Barca

PISTACHIO TO FOREST

GREEN

———

Lush, verdant, vibrant and life-affirming, green is a constant in our
lives. Intrinsically linked to the natural world, green can be energy boosting,
mood-enhancing and grounding. Green is the colour of new growth, of
country gardens and meadow fields, deep ancient forests and vast fertile plains.
We long to surround ourselves with optimistic and rejuvenating shades of fresh
grass, zesty lime and decadent emerald. Yet softer shades of sage, olive or pale
mint speak of sanctuary, and a sense of restored balance and well being.

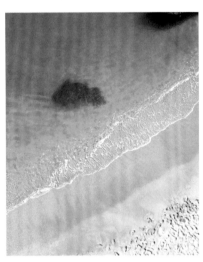

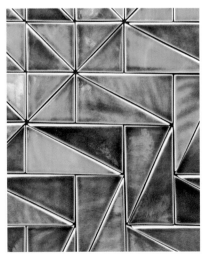

GREEN: PISTACHIO TO FOREST

Left: Greens work well on most materials and finishes, including flat, matt hand-painted wood and high-shine and translucent glazes and glasswork. Decorative motifs, curled ironwork and painted mosaics are inspired by the natural world. Try using an accent of soft brick red or pale apricot against a green backdrop.

Right: Blur the boundaries between inside and outside, bring nature into your home to create an oasis of privacy and peace.

Tropical greens call to mind balmy days spent relaxing in sun-dappled courtyards. In hot climates, living spaces tend to spill out into open-air rooms, patios and terraces, and these outdoor spaces are often filled with terracotta pots of glossy-leaved plants and abundant flowers, creating a sense of tranquillity and closeness to nature. Fountains and water channels running along tiled floors help to abate the heat of the midday sun. The green colour family offers us the chance to reconnect with

Mother Earth, bringing the outdoors into our homes. We can live in harmony with nature and use its dominant colour to breathe new life into tired spaces. Greens are wonderful blended and layered together in a single living space. Cooling, peaceful and harmonious shades of green – such as pistachio, jade, mint and seafoam – work effortlessly together on a multitude of surfaces, ranging from glossy ceramic tiles to chalky matt paintwork.

It is wonderful to fill our living spaces with real plants and to take inspiration from the shades of green of the changing seasons. Cactus colours can inspire a perfect palette of softened greyed-greens. Add a touch of springtime to your kitchen with clean and clear mints or pale leaf greens. These pretty pale greens work well for woodwork and ceramics – you can even source electrical appliances in mint and pistachio finishes.

Above and right: Bring the outdoors in, using succulents and cacti, ferns and hyacinths. A green colour scheme is timeless and easy to live with; we instantly feel rooted when we are surrounded by greens in the home. Draw on different shades of green throughout the year: painted surfaces can be soft and matt like the underside of a sage leaf, while hard finishes, such as flooring, recycled glass and heavy glazed planters, can be sourced in beautiful tints of green.

Left: Green rejuvenates and replenishes the spirit. No matter where we live, rural or urban, we are naturally drawn to the colour green. Create your own oasis of jungle leaves using bold digital leaf print wallpaper – this one is in the heart of Istanbul, Turkey – or try juxtaposing a solid expanse of vibrant green against graphic black-and-white patterns. A minimal flash of bright red is an unexpected and fabulous accent on a solid green wall.

Right: Introduce rich green textiles to enliven an area, as in this hotel's stunning outdoor lounge area on an island in the Mexican Caribbean.

Incorporating natural materials in the home is a simple way to soften our unnatural habitats. Undyed, unpainted and raw wood, rattan or bamboo have a wonderful warm, golden natural coloration and pleasing textures that work especially well with greens. Celebrate organic materials, with exposed wooden ceiling beams, natural seagrass flooring and jute lampshades. To avoid a scheme becoming too rustic, contrast the traditional with contemporary digital zigzag patterns or highly polished table tops.

When playing with pattern and wallpaper, keep your colour palette focused and limited. Modern design and new printing technologies give us the option to bring oversized printed materials into our living spaces. Huge banana leaves or lush jungle greens create an interior that is both fun and vibrant. Use large-scale pattern and decoration on a single wall or juxtapose solid colour on a wall with monochrome artwork and pattern accents.

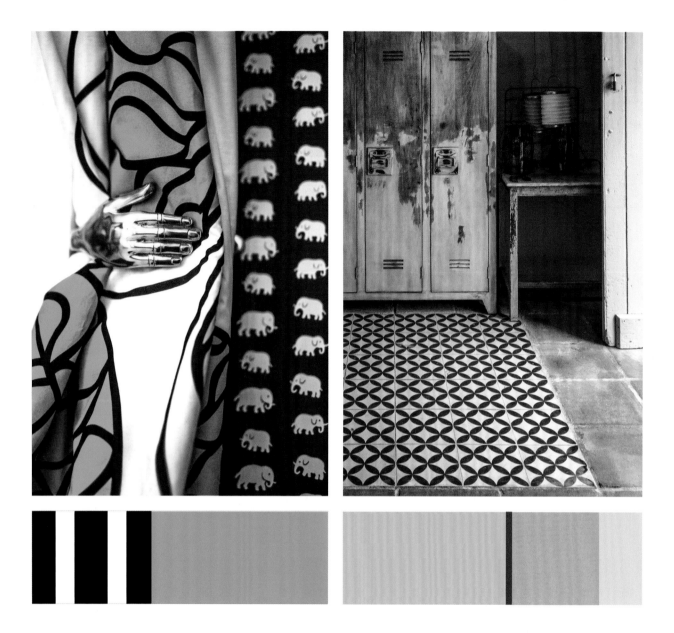

Pattern and graphic decoration add focus and depth to a room. Geometric pattern can lift an otherwise simple palette of colours – here, greens are successfully combined with monochrome. A simple repeat graphic pattern is bold, modern and yet somehow timeless. Pattern can also give an unexpected twist to a scheme, elevating the space and creating layers of visual interest.

A classic black-and-white pattern never looks dated or out of place and introducing natural, soothing greens softens the overall look. Contrasting the paintwork colours with the symmetrical, geometric pattern of the floor tiles creates a striking effect. Colour combinations need to be kept to a minimum, just two or three shades working together, to allow the pattern to take centre stage.

Pattern is no longer reserved for cushions and traditional floral motifs. Modern design solutions are just as likely to see pattern being introduced into our homes in new and energizing ways. Try mixing pattern across wall coverings and floor tiles, and play around with scale; juxtaposing different sized versions of the same design motifs is effective.

Left and above: These greens are mid-toned, striking and vibrant, ranging from peashoot to olive – they need to be used in a focused and well-thought-out scheme. A bright grass green is an unexpected and uplifting flash here. Dark charcoal grey or black outlines define the pattern in these rooms, while warming, washed terracotta floor tiles soften the contrasting colours throughout.

Use mid-tone shades of green in the bedroom or living room. The first shoots of spring inspire clean, clear tones that have a zingy note. Herbaceous greens, such as spearmint and peashoot, used on either walls or furnishings will invigorate any space. These fresh, light colours create an effect that is at once uplifting and inviting.

Left and above: Green can work wonders when used in unexpected areas of a room; try it on a bedroom ceiling to add interest to a surface you first see upon waking, or as a colour-saturated solution to create a peaceful place in which to unwind and freshen up.

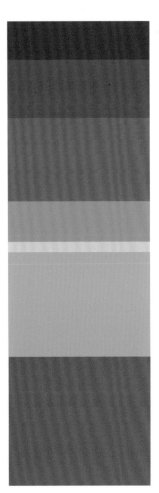

Greens can be used to spectacular effect. Precious tones of bright emerald and rich jade add depth and enliven any surface. Consider how these saturated, jewel-like colours can be introduced into a room scheme. Sumptuous fabrics, such as velvets and silks, will introduce opulence but can also help to soften a space. Gloss paintwork, metallic surfaces, vintage glassware and gleaming ceramic glazes all emphasize the luxury of these shades. What is striking here is that the brightest emerald green colour, normally reserved for an accent, dominates the room.

Pinks and greens work beautifully together, creating an often surprising and refreshing colour palette. Flat-painted pale pink walls provide a perfect backdrop to gleaming green furniture, allowing it to take centre stage. Plush velvets can be reminiscent of theatre seating or lavish restaurant interiors but, used cleverly, this luxurious fabric can be brought coolly into the twenty-first century. Such a scheme isn't simply about colours, it is also about mixing up textures to create a space with interesting layers of contrast.

Emerald green is a bold colour to use in furnishings or curtains in order to create a dramatic living area. Large rooms with high ceilings can be transformed through the adventurous use of saturated colours. Pay little heed to the saying 'blue and green should never be seen' and experiment with intense and dazzling layers of rich greens and deep inky blues.

Left: Flamboyant pattern and decoration dominate the walls and floor. Each element is pulled together through the continual use of bright emerald.

Above: These soft olive green walls work as a subdued canvas on which to add flashes of brighter green textiles.

Following pages: Go for a truly maximalist finish and fill your space with enchanting layers of colour, pattern and decoration. Verdant greenery blends effortlessly from interior to exterior.

In many cultures the colour green is synonymous with wealth, prosperity and luxury. Intensely rich greens are intrinsically linked to a sense of abundance and success. In nature the vast spectrum of the colour green in all its wonderful shades means health, growth and renewal. Let this inspire you to embrace the great many positive attributes linked to the colour green.

Kingfisher, hummingbird or peacock greens have a blueish cast. Inspired by the iridescent gleam of a flash of green feather, these shades glint and shimmer in the light. Layer them together to create a palette of decadent greens. Choose materials and finishes that reflect and play with light – a lustrous velvet, a glass-topped cabinet, a highly polished varnish or a metallic paint finish.

The natural world can so often inform pattern, decoration and furnishings. Peacock-coloured botanical themes can be enhanced with a metallic shimmer. Use gold leaf to cover a ceiling or an alcove, and position your lighting to pick out the gleaming surfaces.

Left: Wallpaper and fabric designs are frequently inspired by flora and fauna. Foliage creeps across a dining room wall and flower forms are mutated in woven metallic threads. Nature is transformed into sublime intricate materials in this voluptuous palette of greens.

Above: A botanical scheme can be outlined by using black lacquer or ebony woodwork, black glass table tops and brass fixtures and fittings.

The darkest of greens, close to black but just one step removed, is a shade that is intense and enduring, like an evergreen forest. Using such a dark shade for a large space might seem ambitious, but actually it creates a sense of intrigue and drama. Soft lighting and the matt finish build a theme of classic style and elegance. For balance, keep the floor and work surfaces pale and incorporate decorative touches that are orderly and simple.

Left and above: The Japanese call this deep forest colour *chitose midori*, meaning 'Thousand Years Green'. Here, it lends personality and confidence to a large dining kitchen. The single colour – used across the walls and the woodwork for the doors, island unit and display shelving – creates a sophisticated backdrop to the daily business of cooking and eating.

"It was June, and the world smelled of roses. The sunshine was like powdered gold over the grassy hillside." Maud Hart Lovelace

BUTTERCUP TO TURMERIC

YELLOW

———

Yellow is the colour of sunshine, spring daffodils and fields full of sunflowers. Yellow can be fresh and zingy like lemons or as sweet and delicious as honey. Rich, exotic and elemental, this is the colour of ochre, sulfur, amber and saffron. Yellow is rebellious and carefree, uplifting and energy-boosting, filling us with unadulterated joy and exuberant optimism. It is also rich and luminous, the colour of enlightenment. In essence, yellow is a celebration of life.

Left: A white wall is filled with a riot of colour and pattern, a joyous collection of eye-catching art and treasures. The bright sunshine yellow cabinet is the perfect frame for the objects gathered on its shelves, drawing the eye in and creating a sense of order where there appears to be none.

Right: Incorporate yellow in unexpected ways to add an upbeat edge to a space. In a dining room or home office, an entire yellow wall may be too overwhelming, instead use yellow as an accent colour to pick out details. Paint a single dining chair yellow, or choose a bright yellow desk lamp for your office.

Following pages: A sun-filled street in Campeche, Mexico, is drenched in bright warming light and contrasted with beautiful shades of blue to echo the cloudless skies above.

Yellow can elevate a space, breathing life and joy into any room. The bright glow of sunshine yellow will lift your spirits whatever the weather outside. There is no need to be too serious with colour; you should have fun when decorating your home and follow your imagination. We travel through life collecting objects and filling our homes with treasures. These precious things can inspire a riotous palette of hot and vivacious colours – think of acid yellow, neon peach and daring magenta.

If you feel a little colour-shy, start off by introducing a few bright accents into a neutral scheme. Yellow looks fantastic against a clear white background. Choose some super-bright printed cushions, or find inspiration in a dynamic, brightly coloured graphic art print – perhaps display this in a colourful frame too. Then, if you like the effect, try picking out the woodwork in a room with an eye-popping candy tone, or simply paint a door frame in zingy citrus yellow.

Yellows work wonders as secondary or accent colours in an otherwise fairly neutral scheme. All hues of grey happily partner yellow, from pale, smoky-grey walls to darker slate fabrics and flooring. Choose a dandelion yellow to create a pop of colour against a grey or black-and-white scheme. In a living room, use darker layers of deep ochre, caramel or mustard, framed with charcoal or indigo blue.

Above and right: Notice how the choice of surface finish and fabrics in a room scheme can affect colours. The metallic and high-shine cocktail accessories add a touch of golden glamour to a corner of a living room, mixing colours from caramel to bright gold, brass to amber. Part of the magic of yellow is that when it is given a metallic finish, it resembles gold. Hint at luxury by featuring coloured metals, or polished golden glass, from rose gold to brass, in your room design.

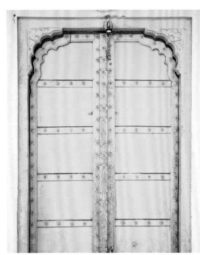

YELLOW: BUTTERCUP TO TURMERIC

Left: Yellow immediately catches the eye and instils a sense of cheerfulness. A yellow painted window frame of a coastal cottage in England, amber trade beads in a Middle Eastern bazaar, a bright yellow dress spotted on the streets of New York and a citrus-yellow wall in South America all offer a flash of welcome colour against a grey backdrop.

Right: Bring vibrant shades indoors to liven up your interior. Sulfur yellow, rich spiced terracotta and palm-leaf green echo the exotic colours found in the garden of this Mexican villa.

For centuries, brightly coloured paint or dye was only available to the wealthy. Now everyone can afford the luxury of bringing vivid colour into their lives. Yellow woodwork, golden fabric for soft furnishings or an accent of amber-patterned wallpaper are small details that will constantly bring a smile to your face. Celebrate the effects of yellow in your home, and use glowing, golden surfaces and materials to light up dark spaces.

Rich sulfuric yellow is the most welcoming of colours to use in a dark entrance hall, or to paint a front door. The entrance to a home is the first thing we see, so flood it with a welcoming embrace of colour; your home will appear sunny and inviting. 'Advancing' tones in the range between red and yellow are both exciting and invigorating. Use these enlivening shades to create a stimulating atmosphere and fill the space with vigour and energy.

Combine complementary shades from the fiery side of the spectrum, such as spiced yellow and burnt orange, using these powerful, rich colours to bring warmth to a room. Choose mouth-watering tones of butterscotch, toffee and honeycomb, mixed together with marmalade, Seville orange and pumpkin pie. Be inspired by the fruits of nature to create a deliciously intense palette.

If choosing hot orange or vibrant orchid pink as your pop colour, the yellow background shade should have a reddish or golden tint. The deep intensity of the golden yellows is exaggerated and enhanced through accents of other colours from the fire family. Greenish yellows, lemon, citrus and cooler yellows would sit less comfortably alongside the hot oranges.

These gold-tinged yellows are also highly spiritual colours, associated with temples, meditation and peace. The saffron-coloured robes worn by Buddhist monks, symbolize a sense of humble veneration. The yellow garments of the Hindu gods Vishnu and Krishna represents light and knowledge. Choose your shade of yellow well and it will undoubtedly boost your mood.

Left: Colours inspired by spices such as turmeric, saffron, nutmeg and cinnamon are naturally heartening and warming. Turmeric has many health benefits – it has long been a staple of Ayurvedic medicine – and using such a strong colour in our homes can also be uplifting and good for the soul.

Above: Choose Indian yellow, a rich shade with a deep golden hue, to bring warmth into a darkened stairwell. In a child's bedroom, ochre or deep yellow is a perfect bright wall colour.

Left and right: Using this rich mango colour from floor to ceiling infuses this kitchen with warmth and sunshine. Fill your kitchen with a wealth of golden tones – take inspiration from courgette flowers, sweetcorn, papaya and melon.

The kitchen is the centre of the home, a place where families gather, friends meet, and children play. In the kitchen we work daily to nourish our bodies and fuel our souls. It is vital that this room makes us feel good. Deep yellows can brighten moods and increase energy levels, which is why we love the colour yellow in our kitchens; it really is great for a morning boost of energy. Like a shot of espresso, a bright colour in the kitchen can help to wake us up and feel ready to face the day.

Any kitchen that is starved of natural light would certainly benefit from a blast of hot yellow colour. Choose mango paint on cabinets to fill an entire wall area. Contrasting shades of rich yellow and dark steel blue offer a modern and original palette. It is best not to use these confident colours in equal measure though: one should be an accent and, here, it is the dark blues that fall away, allowing the bright yellow to command all the attention.

Most colours have cultural significance or generally accepted associations. Yellow is globally recognized as signifying light, warmth and happiness. These glowing, orange-tinged yellow courtyard walls reflect the heat of the Mexican sun. Accent golden yellow with pale pink to lighten the intense vibration of the colour, or outline yellows with dark green or a rich mahogany brown.

Left and above: For centuries Mayan people have painted the walls of their houses this deep, warm yellow as a way to offer respect to the sun god, Kinich Kakmó.

Ochre is derived from a natural clay pigment extracted directly from the earth. It ranges in hue from yellow to orange to brown. Pieces of ochre have been found in South Africa that date back seventy-five thousand years. It was used for prehistoric cave paintings and the ancient Egyptians applied it extensively to their tomb paintings. Throughout art history, ochre has been a staple colour.

Mix yellow ochre with other earthy tones, such as umber, terracotta and clay. Warming hues of reddish browns, peppercorn and softened spiced reds work incredibly well against a background of golden ochre. Intricate and detailed woven patterns, embroidery and cutwork on antique throws and cushions inspire a palette rich with gold and red.

Black or dark grey are fantastic contrast colours next to yellow. Try juxtaposing highly decorative textiles sourced from North Africa, Central Asia or India in each colour, preferably mismatched, and notice how beautifully they work together. This rich shade of ochre is seen again and again, on furniture and chairs, bedding and rugs, cushions and curtains.

Left and above: Mix bohemian-style rugs and throws sourced in the souk in Marrakech or a bazaar in Rajasthan. Layer pattern and texture to create a cosy and inviting atmosphere. Use warming colours, which complement each other, all tones with a reddish hue. Hand crafted and artisanal textiles have a wonderful natural quality to them, they tell a story and imbue an interior scheme with a sense of history and belonging.

Occasionally a single colour does all the talking within a room scheme. Here, the same colour has been painted on every wall and even the ceiling. It is a deep, luscious, saturated shade of greenish, golden yellow, like a bottle of the best olive oil. It is a rich and fragrant shade that transforms and changes as the light of the day bounces around the room. The effect is of stepping into a sanctuary, a heart-warming, spirit-cleansing space, as if we are being bathed in a colour and emerging fresh and re-energized.

Modern research has revealed that when our eyes connect with colour, our brains release different chemicals. This reaction really can have an impact on us, on both a physical and an emotional level. This is why it is vital that you choose colours for your home that you truly love, colours which instinctively make you feel happy. These colours are not the same for everyone; trust your own judgement and create a colourful environment that suits you.

"I saw a sunset in Queretaro that seemed to reflect the colour of a rose in Bengal."

Jorge Luis Borges

APRICOT TO COPPER

ORANGE

———

Orange can glow like the embers of a fire, or blaze like a flaming sun sinking below the horizon; it is a colour that burns brightly in the dark of night. Yet orange can also be soft and blushing – the antique powder colour of a pair of silk stockings, or the palest shades of orange blossom, apricot and peach. Orange is earthy like Tuscan terracotta, or the colour of autumn leaves and ripe pumpkin, of burnished copper or the colour of cognac. Orange is nourishing and full of heat: think of ginger, paprika and cinnamon. The colour of tropical cocktails, of carnivals and marigolds, orange demands to be noticed.

Tangerine, apricot and pale peach work together in a tropical fruit cocktail of intoxicating shades. Layer on top with vibrant accents, from coral to fuchsia pink. Infusing these happy colours in your home invokes a relaxed, friendly atmosphere. Orange colours are said to boost appetite as well as mood, making these colours brilliant to use in a kitchen or dining area.

Left: Clever pops of hot colours jostle for attention against a clean white background. Sunshine yellow is the perfect accent to the hot oranges here.

Above: Pick out architectural detailing in a contrasting bright shade to add a sense of fun. The bright peach on the exterior of a house in Reykjavik, Iceland, is a welcome burst of vibrancy in this cold, northern environment and contrasts beautifully against the dark grey concrete street. A cherry-red front door further lifts this hot shade and almost glows with intensity.

The paler end of the orange spectrum affords a selection of luxurious and elegant shades, from dusted, chalky plaster, to rusted earthy spice tones. These sophisticated colours prove that orange does not have to be bright, bold and electrified. Powdery cosmetic shades of blush or nude are the perfect foundation colours in a palette. Add vintage charm to your living room or bedroom with tones of peachy coloured plaster, or leave brickwork exposed.

Here, the painted walls have a softly textured finish; no surface is clear or flat. Tones of the same shade are gently smudged one upon the other, giving a tactile, naturally imperfect finish. Choose surfaces and textiles with a low lustre or delicate sheen. Each material should encourage touch, from matt and powdery walls to vintage silk lustre. Mix colours of orange blossom and wild peach with pretty shades of lavender-grey. Lift the scheme with accents of antique gilt, or rose-tinted gold.

Earthy, burnt-orange tones are honest, rustic colours that have adorned homes since time immemorial. Terracotta – literally translated as 'baked earth' – is a key shade, reliable and satisfying. Like the burnt umber shades of Tuscan villas and the rich reddish sienna found in prehistoric cave paintings, these clay colours form a warming, natural environment.

Used since antiquity for flooring and roof tiles, drinking vessels and walls, clay and terracotta are vital components of our built environment. Choosing a palette of these earth-born materials reconnects us with our ancestors, realigns our souls and helps to ground us in nature. These are homely, comforting colours that work well in the kitchen or bathroom, breathing warmth into

these spaces of ritual and cleansing. Materials here are hand-finished and natural. Like the adobe houses of New Mexico or the rammed-earth desert homes of northern Africa, no corner is sharp and no surface is truly flat. It is vital that we continue to bring hand-crafted objects into our homes and to celebrate their imperfections and individuality.

Left: Natural materials are celebrated throughout this Spanish home with olive wood surfaces, woven straw baskets and terracotta tiles. Naive hand-painted flowers on the ceramic dish continue the theme of connection with the natural world.

Above: Rich orange earth tones are used to fashion pots and vessels and to plaster walls all around the world, from South America to India and Africa.

Blue complements orange. Placing these two colours side by side, or using one to accent the other, makes the contrast between them even more intense – like fire and ice, or an oasis of cool tranquillity in the middle of a scorching desert. Tints of blues work beautifully on woodwork against the rich orange walls. Colours blend from indoor spaces to outdoor, as house exteriors are washed in the colours of the setting sun.

Shadow and light add further contrast and trick the eye, turning peach into saturated deeper orange. Layers of glowing sunset shades, from burnt coral to russet, amberglow to canyon, vie for attention. The deep blue of the sky at dusk, or a violet grey-blue of early dawn are vibrant and cooling here, offering a much-needed contrast, with accents ranging from palest blue-tinted-grey to deep denim.

Rather than restricting your scheme to a single bold colour, try using a combination of warming shades to emphasize the overall effect. Layered tones of hot colours work well. Deeper, richer shades of poppy red or marmalade orange appear more full and vibrant when paired with lighter, brighter yellows. Try blending gold, amber and honey, or flame, ginger and saffron for similar impact.

Above: The 'hot' colours of the rainbow are encapsulated in a house in Mexico, blending from red, orange to golden yellow.

Right: Take inspiration from the colourful buildings in the Nyboder district of Copenhagen, Denmark. Here, striking shades play off against one another.

Following pages: Orange isn't always overly bright or vivid. Deep rusted or spiced oranges veer towards the neutral colour family and so can work well for larger expanses of wall.

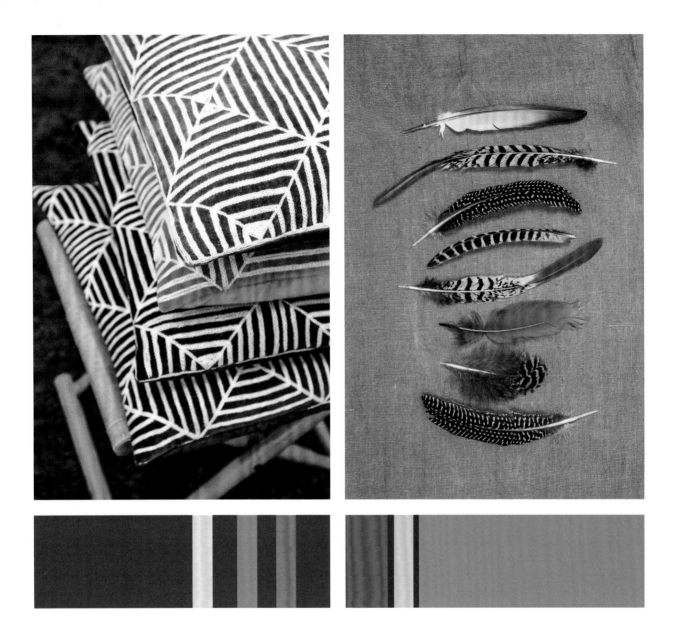

There is a considered ease, a steady pace of genteel natural shades in all these interiors. Glowing orange tones – think of rust or copper, ginger or cinnamon – enliven and warm an otherwise neutral palette of white or warm grey. A bright orange cushion, or a flash of hot Indian marigold orange in a monochrome setting will make the entire scheme feel bright and modern.

Surface and texture can further elevate these accent colours. Neutral and natural materials, including pale wood, undyed wool, parchment and stone can all be lifted and enhanced by a pop of orange, from dark brick, red oxide, to the gentle haze of fading apricot hues. Tones of warm greys and undulating browns blend with timeless confidence to create a pleasing and balanced effect.

Tinted, golden, glazed, bronzed or patinated materials and finishes further enhance these colours. With time, varnished wood and hammered metals take on a unique and deeper hue, a more intense patina. The mellow reflection of copper adds its gleam, and vintage leather or a flagstone floor will develop a polished sheen through generations of wear.

Left and above: A single, well-chosen object, an eye-catching orange fabric or a rust-coloured vase, can lift an entire room design. From bronze-coloured pheasant feathers to polished metal frames, glazed and gilded surfaces catch the light and provide a welcoming glow.

Left and right: Play with print, combine and contrast motifs and styles, yet always stick to your overarching colour palette. Pick out a single key colour from a printed textile and use this to create a feature wall. Or mix and match coordinating coloured patterns in a playroom or an en-suite bathroom. Combine different patterns in a small room for a touch of fun.

For a scheme that is powerful, indulgent and vivid, choose deep shades of orange with a pinkish tint. These are easier on the eye than a fully-saturated true orange, which is often considered too brash. Colour, like pattern, can be used in innovative ways to separate areas and rooms within your home. These colour zones steer the eye from one room to another – a bold orange room leading off a simple grey hallway, for instance, will invite guests into your home.

Do not be afraid to experiment with vibrant print and decorative pattern. Prints can create a strong point of focus in a room, like a bold floral wallpaper restricted to a single area, or this unmissable Indian floral throw on a modern cabin-style bed. If you are still unsure about using bold pattern, use more subtle designs throughout a room scheme. Contrast embroidered textiles, painted woodwork, ornamental rugs and patterned accessories in complementary and tonal colours.

Left: Consider new colour palettes for a bathroom scheme. We want to feel pampered in the bathroom, creating our own private spa. Warming shades of autumnal oranges are nurturing and indulgent, the perfect choice for a relaxed and cosy bathing experience.

Right: A graphic, monochrome colour scheme is sharp and modern, but can appear cold, too. Inject an instant flash of warmth through orange accessories or textiles.

When working a hot colour into your design, sticking to a very simple colour palette shows real confidence. Use bold blood orange as your main focus colour and keep all other walls and details in pale and neutral shades. Shades of white, or pale greys like smoke or feather, offer a cool backdrop to bright orange. Natural finishes, from scrubbed wood to chalk paint and stone surfaces, offer warming neutrals that will come alive once paired with these hot fiery shades.

A cool palette of natural grey tints can be completely transformed through the introduction of a pop of hot mandarin or firecracker orange. Monochromatic schemes of, black and white, or charcoal grey and off-white, are classic colours to use in pattern and decoration within your home. Choose organic forms or botanical drawings in duotones for a softly elegant and timeless use of pattern, enlivening them with the glowing warmth of your accent colour.

Above and far right: These blazing orange tones light up dark corners and create evocative settings. Brightly coloured runners can be used to great effect as a carpet on a neutral staircase. Deep marmalade and tiger orange are intricately blended in artisanal textiles and woven rugs. The pattern and ornament is accentuated with bold details in black and ivory.

In the natural world, deep orange signals the changing seasons, as the cool greenery of summer turns to the burnished glow of autumn. Orange represents the last of nature's harvest. Homely and restorative, these glowing shades are gorgeous all year round, but in the autumn months they lend themselves perfectly to cosy throws and richly embroidered floor cushions.

A deep, dark setting allows the colours of copper beech and glowing amber to shine out. Like a fabulous dessert, we can layer mouth-watering hues of burnt caramel, toffee pudding and glossy chocolate sauce together. Here, the dense, espresso-coloured walls recede, allowing elaborate pieces of furniture to take centre stage.

Rich, deep, and captivating colours can be brought to life through the application of sensual, shimmering and lustrous surface finishes. Copper-toned velvets catch the light and glossy metallics gleam luxuriously. A clever use of feature lighting can cast a honey-hued light throughout a space, warming and steeping a room in these evocative colours.

Left and right: Polished brass lighting, vintage mirrors and smoky tinted glass all add a touch of retro glamour to a space. Metallic surfaces and luxe indulgent fabrics are lifted through imaginative accent lighting. Glowing vintage fairground bulbs sparkle and twinkle.

"Bright reds – scarlet, pillar-box red, crimson or cherry – are very cheerful and youthful. There is certainly a red for everyone." Christian Dior

SCARLET TO RUBY

RED

Red is arresting, exciting, dynamic and unashamed – a confident, powerful colour. Red makes us stop and look; it is provocative, glamorous and dramatic. Hot-blooded, fiery and full of passion, reds are unapologetically primal and intoxicating. Reds suggest elemental energy and represent temptation, happiness, luck and love. In China, red is associated with good fortune. In India, red symbolizes joy, life and creativity.

This courtyard exemplifies how hue and surface texture play a significant part in the effectiveness of colour combinations. The mouth-watering berry red, rippling with nuances and textures, is complemented perfectly by bright azure green. The natural quality of faded or washed red is ideal for interiors. Reds with a blueish tint, or a darker, wine-coloured hue, recede beautifully to create a bold yet classic look.

Left: A sun-filled courtyard in Mérida, Mexico, plays with cool and warm colours with the deep rich softened red on the back wall bringing the green on the side wall to life.

Above: Take inspiration from these antique subway tiles, found in a flea market in New York. The aged texture softens the reds, brown and blues together.

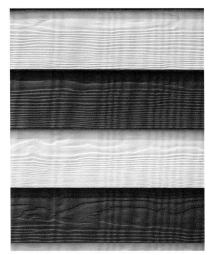

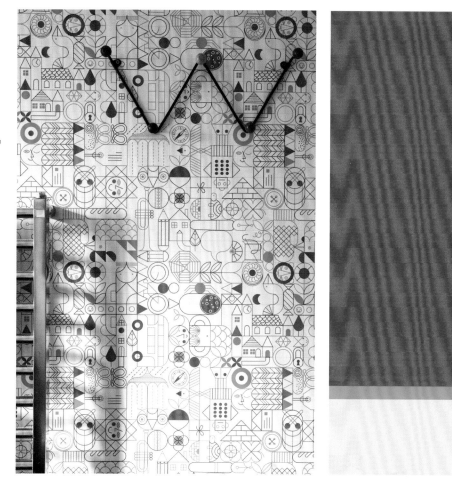

Left: Introduce red into your colour scheme through pattern and decorative elements. Look to the British seaside for inspiration. Stripy deckchairs and beach umbrellas, beach huts and sticks of rock. Pattern can be unfussy like a chequerboard repeat found in a brightly woven floor mat in Tarifa, southern Spain, or simplistic and linear, as seen in this wooden fan. If you are feeling adventurous, inject a space with more elaborate pattern. Tiles are a great way of doing this and you can mix and match in a similar fashion to this mosaic street art spotted in Istanbul, Turkey.

Right: Take inspiration from the red, white and blue theme for a bathroom or kitchen, with naive graphic wallpaper. Combine with fun striped textiles.

Following pages: A deep scarlet hue is used to flood this hallway, covering every surface – woodwork, doors and ceiling – and leading us on into a light-filled bedroom.

To keep the look fresh and modern, use the tried-and-tested combination of red, white and blue in clean and unfussy ways. Pure primary shades of red and blue, used together, can feel childlike or naive. Instead, try using different levels and nuances of reds and blues for a more evocative and elegant colour scheme. Choose brighter reds with a vibrant orange-tomato hue, ranging down to levels of pinkish berry or crimson. Try blue with a deeper, darker intensity, and a rich, violet tint.

Finally, the white does not always need to be a pure white – particularly in spaces that receive a lot of direct sunlight. For a softer effect, white with undertones of papyrus or pale cream makes for a less graphic, more sophisticated background to the reds.

Above and right: Treasures from travels, beloved pieces from family and friends, or finds from a local flea market can be carefully arranged and displayed together to create a unique collection with creative appeal.

Many of us are drawn to bright colours, but not everyone is adventurous enough to fill an entire room, top to bottom, with striking shades. A full red colour scheme might not be quite your style; instead try using smaller pieces featuring vibrant accents and flashes of red detail to add personality to an interior, especially if you have a dark or gloomy corner crying out for some attention.

Subtle tones and hues of red can be assertive and exciting, full of energy and vivacity. Carmine, ruby or vermilion are strong reds, powerful, flamboyant, dynamic colour choices, exerting a strength and force wherever you use them. Softer levels of reds, from rusted reds with an earthy tinge, to more gentle, reds verging on pinks are more soothing and calm.

As always, texture, context and surface play their part. Layers of deep reds used on matt, light-absorbing surfaces, result in an exaggerated and intensified colour. The weathered textures of exteriors painted red are gently resilient, offering a timeless welcome to any home. Faded reds exude a sense of settled longevity, a soothing reassurance that these colours will endure for years.

Contrasting colours and accents of high-shine and reflective surfaces add a touch of glamour, and enhance rouged tones. A clean glossy glaze on a cool ceramic delivers an immaculate surface, which is both smooth and self-contained. Gloss paint woodwork, red lacquer or red glass lighting exaggerate and intensify these built-up layers of reds and berries.

Left and above: These images are steeped in strong and saturated colour; we are surrounded by rich and resonant reds. Blood-red colours are comforting and cocooning on a deeply subconscious level. Choosing red will transform a space into a heart-melting, voluptuous interior, simply filled with love.

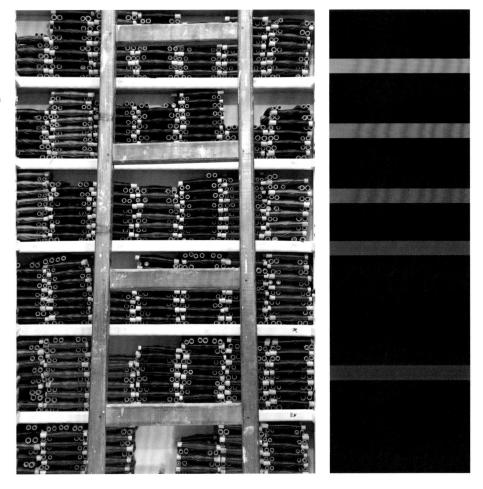

Reds make a wonderful choice for breakfast rooms and dining rooms – they are energizing and add a sense of drama, luxury and occasion. Red is also a colour known to stimulate appetite and encourage debate. A perfect backdrop for any dinner party! Uncertain about painting an entire room red? Then introduce an accent red instead; a simple, glossy red door is an arresting alternative to painting all four walls, encouraging one to step through into the room beyond. Be sure to choose deep, dense shades of red, like Chinese lacquer work, if you are opting for a high-sheen surface. Brighter shades run the risk of a cheaper, more plastic-looking finish. Choosing reds may leave us as overwhelmed as children in a candy store, mesmerized by the vast array of options on offer. From luscious raspberry to lipstick, from striking vermilion to rich port, the possibilities are seemingly endless. But there is a red for everyone, so be brave and experiment with this fantastically versatile colour; you may well fall in love with it.

Red responds energetically when set against darkened, ink or grey backgrounds. A flash of ruby against midnight-blue or dark coral red with deep shadowy black is an intense and vivid combination. Bold pops of red either absorb or reflect light in a darkened dining room. Combine and contrast surfaces such as polished glass and plush textiles against super-matt-painted panel walls.

Above: The high gloss finish on the circular table in this decadent dining room exaggerates the rich and sumptuous contrast of the reds against the dramatic blackened wall colour. Other pieces of red furniture and ornaments continue to pop and zing throughout the space.

Right: The rusted reds in the charming fish-graphic wallpaper, from Cole & Son, are highlighted and accentuated by the raven-black background. A curated collection of books, mimicking the coral reds of the pattern, enhances the scheme.

Left and right: Mix bold and vibrant shades of vermilion, claret, geranium and tomato, creating a saturated palette of colours. Fill your living room with sumptuous velvets and rich softened surfaces that absorb these vibrant colours. Keep pattern to a minimum when decorating with such fiery shades, opt for large-scale colour blocking and simplistic, graphic shapes to keep the effect contemporary.

Clashing shades of red and pink were once considered a fashion disaster, but those days of strict colour rules (and of doing as we are told) are long gone. Sometimes, colours that you might not expect to get along actually bring out the best in each other, creating the most exciting of palettes. Bright tomato red and magenta pink are seductive colours in their own right, but when put together they are transformed from ordinary to magnificent, from everyday to luxurious. A shocking pink velvet chair is completely at home against a backdrop of alluring reds. Pinkish tinted geranium red is levelled, subdued and balanced, through the addition of dark burgundy or claret reds. Always trust your own vision and instinct when choosing colours to cherish and live with. Be bold in your personal colour choices. After all, you are the one who is going to live with it. Pick colours you have fallen in love with entirely, colours you want to be surrounded by for years to come.

"[Pink is] bright, impossible, impudent, becoming, life-giving, like all the lights and the birds and the fish in the world together, a colour of China and Peru, but not of the West – a shocking colour, pure and undiluted." Elsa Schiaparelli

WILD ROSE TO RASPBERRY

PINK

———

From the hushed tones of ballet slipper and soft bubble gum through to energetic fuchsia and dramatic magenta, the spectrum of pinks is varied, rich and abundant. Considered a boys' colour in Victorian times, pink subsequently became associated with femininity and all things sentimental, romantic and girly. Modern pinks, though, have come to represent female empowerment and strength, and they command a presence in design like never before. Sugary pinks range from barely-there marshmallow to the sweetest candy, while more shocking pinks are bold, luscious and provocative.

Use pale tints of dusted plaster in bedrooms and bathrooms. Avoid baby pink, or anything too sickly-sweet, and choose antique pinks reminiscent of your grandmother's face powder. Echo the colour of a freshly plastered wall; matt, flat and flawless. Layer textures in understated hints of pink, from nude to blush. Contrast these softly chalky layers with metallic details; aged copper or rose gold work perfectly.

Left and above: Delicate hints of pinkish powder or plaster are smudged, greyed-off, and lay the perfect ground on which to build your colour palette. Use with lightweight tones of biscuit, vanilla cream and dusted lavender, all colours that blend seamlessly. A hand-crafted feel pervades the materials used, from natural chalk paints to Irish crochet, to hand-screened English wallpaper from Cole & Son.

Twilight pink is the most delicate shade, quiet, self-contained, the touch of peach warm with promise. This is the colour of clouds just as the sun is setting, an elusive glow permeating the sky. Such subtlety and assuredness in a room reads as distinctly grown-up – calmed, sophisticated pinks with a gender-neutral appeal. Pale, powdery pinks can be confident colours, especially when grounded by dove grey. This classic combination draws pink into a more contemporary space, enabling colour to stand alone.

Keep surfaces clean and clear, using only the simplest decoration, and avoid pattern here as the colours speak for themselves. Cool urban greys steer this scheme from becoming too feminine or sweet, adding a more masculine composure. Simple, clean interiors benefit from softer colours that exude a welcoming warmth. Adding familiar, natural materials and textures will introduce tones of pale wood, seagrass and cord, underpinning and lifting the pale colour scheme.

153

Left and right: Colour inspiration is all around us. From striped pinks melted beautifully into a raspberry-ripple palette against weathered wood, luminous threads, tight and silky, contrasting with worn floorboards, to bare plastered walls and decorative floral tiles. Even a homely pile of knitted blankets can suggest colour combinations; here, many different shades can be seen, from seashell to rose quartz, sandy blush to rhubarb.

Nothing in these images is completely smooth or glossy. The walls are unadorned bare plaster and materials are tactile and multi-faceted. Powdery textures and dry, dusted finishes absorb these delicate pinks. Choose sophisticated surface effects: chalky, matt paint, natural marbling and pink-tinted stone. Introduce pattern minimally, and in unexpected ways. To avoid a look that is overly nostalgic, tread cautiously when introducing a floral pattern into a pink-based scheme and instead source botanical shapes and floral patterns that are simplistic, refined and subtly faded. Contemporary manufactured surfaces, such as polished quartz, sand-blasted painted wood panelling or glazed plaster walls all offer pink expanses that are both refined and textural. For a modern and considered interior, one with subtle hints of the seductive and alluring, choose softer textiles and furnishings to complement these gentle delicate pinks.

Dusky pinks are loaded with romance; they appear in myriad forms and we fall in love with them season after season. They present the possibility of escape into worlds full of poetry and desire, hedonism and languid pleasure, imagined interiors of Venetian merchants' houses, intimate salons, afternoons full of warm light and whispers. This palette is packed with rose-tinted, powdered, perfumed, floral shades. From gentlest blush through to wild rose and geranium. Choose wisely though, as a pink palette can tip easily from the sublime to the sentimental, from the courageous to the self-indulgent. Applied with care, these colours can elevate the most ordinary, everyday items into things of beauty, making each moment special. Use pink-tinted teacups at the breakfast table, fill vases

with blossoms and peonies, experiment with fabrics and wall coverings and feathery finishes that play with the light from a nearby window. Indulge all the senses in a pink interior; introduce low atmospheric lighting, use room fragrance and candles, pour a glass of coppery-pink wine, curl up on your chaise lounge and soak up the soft sounds of evening as they close around you.

Left: An evening stroll along the canals in Venice, Italy, inspires a palette of sun-kissed plaster pinks. Combine tones of peach nectar, seashell, apricot and rose cloud, against a background of inky lagoon grey-green to recreate this magical setting.

Above: A beautiful ostrich feather lamp and an impeccably curated collection of curiosities and luxuries evoke a bygone era of opulence and grandeur.

Always consider the quality of natural light when you explore colour options for a particular space in your home. As the day progresses, so the light alters from clear to diffuse, harsh to dazzling, moving between white, blue and yellow tones or softening to a pinkish-hued stillness. Warm, golden summer evenings carry with them a honeyed-pink glow. Interiors that depend heavily on natural light are more effective when they blend outside and inside through shapes, form and colour.

Natural surfaces, curves and fabrics should make the most of adaptable colour schemes that capture, blend and enhance the different qualities of light as it shifts throughout the day. Hazy pink palettes bring to mind lazy summer evenings, nostalgic dreams of painted wooden houses and colonial rooms with sparse, broad floors, tall windows flung wide. Rooms are calm and languid, the epitome of a cool, serene haven in which to escape the heat of the day.

Pinks do not have to be childish, sweet or naive – they can be clear, slick and graphic, challenging preconceptions. Soft greens and pinks look great together. Try a flash of sharp-edged contrast colour with a linear form or pattern to build a contemporary pink scheme. An explosion of citrus lime or lemon, or a burst of brightest violet blue provides an unexpected, joyous flash.

Left: Use graphic inspiration and pattern, to create a unique and striking statement as with this Cole & Son wallpaper. Chose motifs with a strong fine outline, in contrasting cool shades of greens and blues.

Above: Pink is a punchy colour choice for the exterior of your home. Whether it confronts the English climate or a hot Indian summer, pink extends a warm welcome.

Left: Tropical pink walls are emboldened by their colour companions. Here, a flash of brilliant sunshine yellow within an interior archway chases away the dark to create a bright and inviting entrance in Mérida, Mexico.

Right: Take inspiration from this colourful street corner in Mexico. Mix bubblegum pink with cobalt and a pop of mango yellow – a joyful combination for a children's playroom.

Following pages: A flash of bright pink in a walled garden creates the perfect backdrop to the deep green foliage and palms.

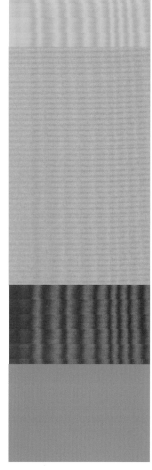

Bright tropical pinks make us smile, lift our spirits and energize other colours around them. The pinks in this group are fresh and zingy, packed with punch. These are the colours of South American and Mexico, of Luis Barragán – the celebrated Mexican architect who dared to use shocking pink on the walls of his Modernist buildings. Choose bright pink for a feature wall in a kitchen or living room to see how the colour lifts the atmosphere of the interior.

Paradise pinks can also offer a welcome respite from the drab greys of an urban environment. Modern urban architecture and street art are inspiring, using bright colours on a grand scale – oversized pinks can be uplifting and powerful. Be confident in your choices at home; bright pinks work as well on garden and exterior walls as they do inside. Use clever contrasts to bring focus and attention to key architectural features. Choose colour partners that glow together and exaggerate one another.

Diana Vreeland, editor of American *Vogue*, famously stated: 'Pink is the navy blue of India.' Indian colour schemes present an inescapable rainbow at every occasion – from the beautiful chaos of Holi, the coloured-powder festival that welcomes the coming of spring, to the vivid red, pink or deep orange worn by brides. Bright colour is celebrated; everywhere one turns there are punchy, attention-grabbing pops of powerful and clashing colour. Contrasting combinations partner strong magenta with acid greens, or artificial frosting colours of strawberry candy against bold blue, green and yellow. These pinks are so vivid and intense they almost appear fluorescent. The brightest of pinks, the most shocking of all colours, are brilliantly powerful and unashamedly domineering.

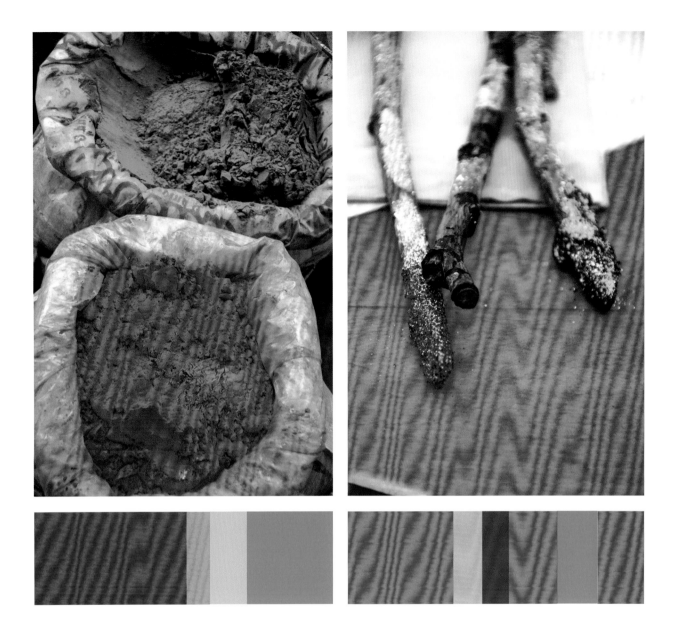

Left: India inspires with bright and celebratory colour. Every type and style of home is adorned and decorated in exuberant, happy clashing tones, like this pink and green doorway in Pushka, Rajasthan.

Above: In Jaipur, Rajasthan's capital, magenta and emerald green powders are ready and waiting for Holi. Violet or blueish pinks combine and contrast with verdant, luscious blueish greens, colours that vibrate perfectly against one another.

Above and right: Saturate your home with a single flamboyant colour for a sensational and decadent affect. Mouthwatering shades of berry pink will enrich your space; these are perfect colours for living and dining areas. Accent bold bright pink with neutral accessories and furnishings, choose off-white, greys and black to allow the colour to stand centre stage.

Saturated raspberry shades can be fun and eccentric, offering a more thoughtful and original choice than reds for doors, walls and fittings. Deeper choices of richly toned cerise and darker berries are decadent and grown-up while still retaining a sense of playfulness. Use these drenched colours with deep greys and blacks, or against a touch of gold for pure opulence.

PINK: WILD ROSE TO RASPBERRY

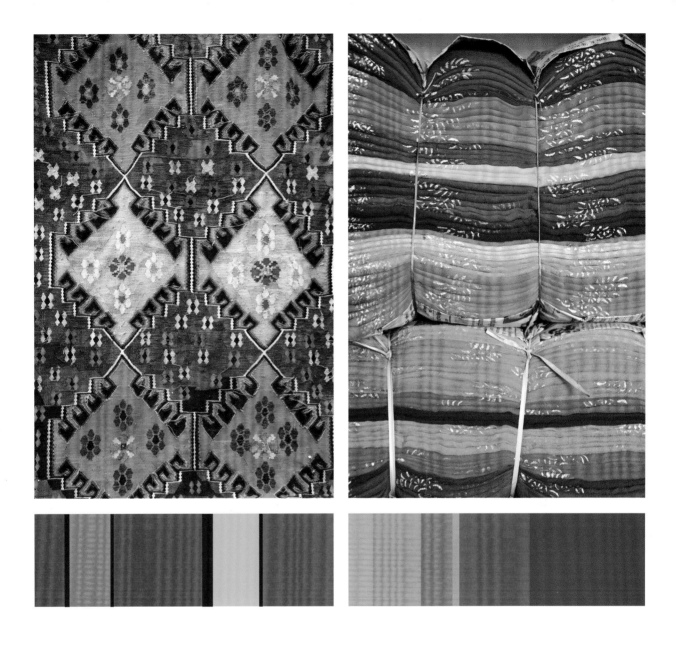

Quirky combinations of pattern and apricot- or coral-pinks create an irreverent but homely scheme, full of nostalgia. To bring this scheme together, tones of peachy pinks are used to complement one another. Mix and match pattern on walls and floors, as well as in textiles. Try a pop of bold coral in unexpected places, such as a fireplace surround, to create contrasting woodwork, or even on the ceiling.

Left: A stripped-back bedroom in an artist's home uses a clever mix of vintage wallpaper with layers of new and unexpected colour.

Above: Richly patterned rugs from Turkey or decorated sari fabrics from India add deep and everlasting splashes of colour.

Pink doesn't always need to dominate a scheme to make its presence known. Against deep, rich colours, such as charcoal or inky blue, or the deepest shade of azure green, dusky pinks and poppy or bright tomato reds will fizz and resonate. The darkened backdrop allows these colours to express themselves with a sense of drama, like dancers on a stage set. Pink is the centre of attention, yet still elegant and graceful; these pinks are neither overbearing nor showy. For this kind of scheme, choose dusty, bruised, or powdery pinks. Favour those with reddish, terracotta or peachy tones, or flattened pinks blended with a touch of grey. These colours could almost be lifted from a make-up artist's palette. Densely woven wools and antique velvets absorb light and enhance the richness of a colour, creating a voluptuous effect that is both striking and refined. These pinks are sophisticated and sensual, rich, flattering colours that bring a strong sense of quiet style and grace to any interior.

"Soon it got dusk, a grapey dusk, a purple dusk over tangerine groves and long melon fields; the sun the colour of pressed grapes, slashed with burgundy red, the fields the colour of love and Spanish mysteries." Jack Kerouac

VIOLET TO FIG

PURPLE

———

Purple is the colour of daydreams, flights of fancy and fairy tales, of mystery and magic. A regal colour, purple is associated with hierarchy, hedonism, indulgence and privilege, recalling imperial Rome and historical Japanese nobility. In autumn, trees and hedgerows are heavy with the weight of purple fruit – elderberry, blackberry, sloe, plum and damson – laden with rich juice. Floral mauves adorn the woodlands – violets, pansies and foxgloves. Paler tones evoke heavily scented blooms, with fragrant perfume ranging from sugary Parma violet to the clean botanical notes of lavender and lilac.

Left and right: Lavender and blue-tinted pastel lilac tones are cooling and tranquil. Sitting somewhere between dusted pink and pale blue, these shades are muted, subdued and amiable. Grey-toned levels of mauve blend into the background and are now seen as a tinted neutral, a calm and composed background colour.

In Victorian England, mauve and lavender were adopted as colours for half-mourning; along with grey, they provided a gentle (but still respectable) return to colour after a year of wearing black, known as 'deep mourning'. Mauve's association with women of a certain age continues to this day; lavender drawer liners, mauve floral blouses and purple rinses are all part of the cliché. But younger generations are reclaiming violet-tinted, lavender and lilac pastel shades for themselves by embracing them in clothing and hair colour alike. In the home try to avoid pinkish lavender tones; unless you are looking for a specifically sweet effect, reserve such colours for the nursery. Grey-toned, more blueish lilac shades are clean and fresh. Bruised and subdued, dusted powdery tones of heather and mulberry partner pared-back shades of grey beautifully. Try layering thistle and purple sage with greenish greys, mulberry and dusted grape with dove or smoked grey.

Flashes of colour add a joyful spark that can uplift any space or object. Time and again we see how modern colour can elevate the most ordinary of objects into items we covet. Kitchen utensils with bright handles, patterned wallpapers with splashes of neon every now and then in the repeat, or vintage items upcycled with a fresh coat of paint. An injection of colour where it's least expected can bring a smile to your face. Purples work well like this; whether you choose bright or soft tones, purples add an inviting, light touch to otherwise neutral spaces. Dark berry colours are sophisticated and exude a sense of opulence. Gentler purples are calming; soft and soothing lavender tones will create a peaceful serenity perfect for a tranquil bedroom, or a busy work room. Think creatively and don't be afraid to use unexpected shades in surprising ways to inexpensively stamp your own personality on to your home environment. Decorating should always be an extension of oneself.

Different materials and surfaces can completely transform almost any colour. Lustre, gloss and high shine add a sense of drama. Lavish surfaces from polished marble, to cast metals and radiant, shimmering textiles add luxurious touches to a lounge or dining room. Try offsetting dusted, flat shades of lavender and mauve with transient, gleaming surfaces and metallic foils and threads, which change and glow depending on the light in the room.

Keep your eyes open for inspiration and remember to consider complementary colours to lift a scheme. Nature has an uncanny habit of marrying colours in a way that is both pleasing to the eye and unexpected. Look closely at the structure in a piece of amethyst, a purple form of quartz, with its myriad hues of pinkish lavender to deep violet in glorious harmony, and it's easy to see why a purple interior works so well with gleams of metallic and glass objects.

Left: A clean lavender wall creates a vibrant backdrop for gilded vintage brass uplighter floor lamps that contrast this cool, dreamy colour beautifully.

Above and right: Colour transmutes and shifts within surfaces and materials. Light is absorbed and reflected, creating intense and flat areas in these amethyst purples that change and glow as the light alters.

With more of us living in towns and cities than ever before, it has become increasingly important to consciously seek out and welcome elements of nature into our homes. In the depths of winter, when everything seems dark and dormant, a painted flower or woven leaf feels full of promise. Using botanical prints and imagery engages with our unconscious and deep-rooted need to feel some sort of connection to nature; we respond almost instinctively to such organic forms and shapes, especially when they are combined with energizing and feel-good colours. Nature is a constant, wherever we live, and purple finds its place among the hedgerow flowers, forests, fruits and vegetables, and sometimes in the most unexpected of places; the underside of a leaf, a bruised-looking cloud, or part of a shadow. So adorn your living space with colours and motifs that resonate with our planet and help us to reconnect with the world around us, for a more satisfying and fulfilling life.

Left: A rich ochre-coloured wall in an outdoor courtyard in Hoi An, Vietnam, is the perfect contrast colour for this deep plum chair. Using such bright and intense shades in a garden setting is another way to introduce an unexpected flash of colour into your colour scheme.

Above: A vintage chaise longue is upholstered in saturated linen, the colour of fig skin, rich and sumptuous. The curtain fabric has an ombré effect, as levels of plum from light to dark undulate across the surface.

Smudged fig colours are beautiful in furnishings and as decorative touches. Like red wine or berry jam, materials and objects are as stained as the hands of a vintner, in shades of purple, grape and plum. Deep claret or port colours have the heavy blueish hint of blackberries. Ruby berry tones are intense and still, caressing surfaces steeped and layered with intoxicating colour.

Using rich colours on the walls of a room creates a striking and dramatic backdrop; these deep or 'blackened' purples imbue the space with a real sense of luxury. Choose lustrous fabrics, along with glossy and reflective surfaces, to catch the light and enhance the surrounding colours. Juxtapose pale golds and tinted coppery finishes against your purple palette.

The way we use our living spaces may change with the seasons and this, in turn, can affect our colour needs and desires. In winter, these enriching, saturated purples provide a safe, cocooning haven, snug and cosy deep indoors. With the return of summer, colours are lifted and amplified, as natural light streams through the windows, transforming a dark room into a luscious, colour-filled interior.

Deep mulberry shades can create a sense of drama within a room. Like a glamorous 1970s New York nightclub, these colours provide a captivating sense of spectacle. Again, textures such as densely weighted fabrics – in particular velvet – are a perfect partner for dark purples, adding to the sense of luxury and intimacy. Try contrasting matt, light-absorbing fabrics with high-gloss or reflective surfaces.

Left: Subtle, low lighting amplifies the dense blackness of these colours. Contrast dark purples with light-filled pale pinkish plaster walls, and bare washed wooden floorboards, for a more delicate touch.

Above: Be inspired by bar and hotel design, settings that are created to make you feel decadent and indulged. Purple velvet chairs almost glow against this dense midnight-black wall colour. Tinted mirrored surfaces and reflective accent lighting really enhance the timeless effect.

SMOKE TO CHARCOAL

GREY

A perfectly still, grey-toned sky can seem an infinite expanse, an absence of colour stretching outwards. Misty, pale smoke greys create a perfect blank canvas upon which other colours can play. Mid-tone greys of pebble, concrete, steel or pewter – solid and dense – respond strongly to sumptuous surfaces that encourage and enhance their depths. As dusk settles, the dark of night brings deepening greys layering gradually with black, shadow, ash and charcoal sinking into midnight, ebony and raven's wing.

Left: An en-suite bathroom is flooded with natural light when an entire wall is formed by an antique mirror panel. The palest oyster-grey quartz tiles used on the floor and the adjacent wall create a delicate yet exquisite contrast.

Above: The iridescent surfaces of these mid-toned grey metals glow gently like pale, smoky pearls. Set against quiet mid-greys, they lift and enliven a colour palette.

Tarnished metals and the foxed silver of antique mirrors are blemished and oxidized, rich with subtle hints of coppery, greenish notes. It is precisely these imperfections that make these surfaces so appealing, bringing life and lustre to these mid-toned greys. When decorating with foggy, shadowy greys, choose supporting materials with natural depth or imperfections, such as marble, quartz and granite.

Left: Wooden cladding, naturally weathered to grey, merges and roots this home into the bleak and wistful landscape of Dungeness in Kent, UK.

Right: Man-made and natural surfaces fuse and unify over time, becoming one. Roof tiles are shrouded in grey lichen, wooden beams are bleached and greyed by the sea and sun, and flint stone is worn and softened through decades of use.

Silvery greys contain numerous different colour hints, from the gleam of the potter's glaze to weathered wood, slate, flint and tiles. The texture and surfaces of rock, stone, metal and timber are perfected by exposure to the elements, weathered and rubbed away or softly overlaid with patina. We are drawn to the unique qualities of these worn textures and the gentle glow that seems to reside just under their surfaces.

Levels of grey play with tone from light misted moon to dark steel greys, the shades merging and blurring, edges indistinct. Like dappled light emerging through tree branches, or the quiet colours of a twilight sky, these greys are transient, moving between beautiful, patient shades. Greys are timeless, elegant, classic and enduring. They work inside and outside, blending effortlessly in modern or traditional schemes.

Adaptable though they are, you need to pay greys careful attention when selecting shades for your home. A tint or tone in the wrong direction can mean a slip between feeling too warm or too cool. Greys that contain too much lilac or icy blue can make a room feel unwelcoming, and painting all four walls can exacerbate this effect.

Use paint tester pots or fabric samples to study paler, neutral grey tones in different areas of a room. Light, both natural and artificial, will react strongly and sometimes surprisingly with soft neutrals. Lamp light and bulbs with a yellowish quality can transform a subdued grey into an unwelcome and strange pale brown. Similarly, lack of sunlight in a north-facing room can exaggerate the colder properties in a grey.

Spend time with your colour samples to see how they are altered and affected by different lights and different times of the day. Most people prefer to choose greys with a natural hint of cream, string, beige or sand. These colours feel touched by sunlight, warmed and natural, rather than cool and artificial – friendlier, more welcoming and easier to get along with.

Left and above: Soft, neutral grey grounds offer the perfect foundation upon which to build a subtle and calming colour palette. Gentle shades of duck-egg or grey-blue work in harmony with subdued greys and tinted whites. The addition of pale ash wood shelving and the cast of warm yellow light bring a touch of warmth to a cool set of colours.

We need our homes to be havens of rest, providing a refuge from the hustle and bustle of the outside world. We can feel constantly bombarded with images and updates, news and information; the pressure to keep up seems relentless. Our subconscious longs for an uncluttered and restful space, devoid of harshness and brightness, one that is refreshing through its lack of stimulation.

Shades of grey are often employed in hallways and entrances, promising peace and calm when one walks through the door. The right greys for these spaces create an ambiance of quietude, peace and retreat.

Layer light and darker greys to draw the eye inside your home. Fill the entrance hall with a warming, light-filled palette of elegant pearl greys and then choose deeper, more alluring contrasts, from smoke and shadow to charcoal, to define and accentuate spaces within the home.

Left: A spacious hallway in a converted merchant's house in Tarifa, southern Spain, is tiled throughout with cooling grey marble. Shaded rooms and internal courtyards offer respite from the heat of the fierce Andalusian sun. Greys and tinted limewash whites reflect heat and shadowy internal corridors allow a cool breeze to circulate.

Above and right: Try a simple monochrome stripe on the stairs or in your entrance hall. Modern and graphic, black and white is softened when paired with cloud-grey painted woodwork.

Left: Take inspiration from graphic art and packaging design, using dark symmetrical shapes against a pale grey background. Geometric, clean and ordered, everything here has a place and a function within the scheme. Accent colours are picked out and used with caution and subtlety. Here, a golden tone picks out the lampshade, the pillow and the bedside radio.

Right: A flash of grass green jumps out from a geometric pattern on a laundry bag, and is repeated within the simple stack of books below.

Use pale greys to establish your background, then apply linear accents of colour in small-scale, carefully considered placements. Restrained grey tones blended and contrasted on walls, ceilings and woodwork result in a thoughtful scheme that is confident and assured. Employ slightly darker colours on radiators, skirting boards, doors and door frames, and a paler shade on the ceiling. Avoiding whites for this sort of palette means each colour is an eye-pleasing tonal variation.

Brighter, bolder colours should be used in moderation and with care. Use tones to pick out other features in the room, pulling everything neatly together. Keep pattern minimal, with prints of angular shapes and mathematical line used as accent decoration within these simplistic settings. Use the opportunity to have objects that you love on display, those that have perhaps inspired you, such as a favourite bag or the colourful spines of books piled in a tower.

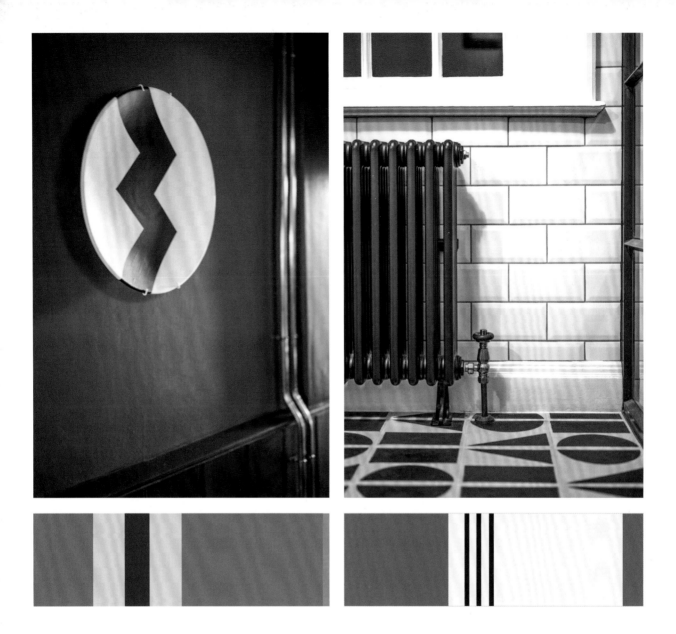

Above: Sometimes the simplest palette and pattern combination can have the most dramatic effect. Here, black-and-white hand-painted ceramic accessories and tiles demand all the attention. Keep the remainder of the space clean and monochrome.

Right: An elegant entrance hall is redefined for the modern era through an enchanting collection of pattern and curious objects. The black-and-white palette draws together the whimsical design, creating a fun yet stylish reception.

Black and white together is striking and timeless. These two simple colours, side by side, never fail to create a graphic, bold and dramatic impact. This classic combination enhances so many spaces and designs. Encourage pattern and decoration in a monochrome scheme to prevent it looking stark or too minimal, or soften the effect by pairing charcoal and bone.

Grey is not an absence of colour; rather it is full of nuance, shade and tone, occupying all the unsung spaces between black and white, carefully filling the corners and owning the edges. Light makes all colour possible – in complete darkness, no colour exists. As in black-and-white photography, we see pattern and definition pick their way through degrees of grey.

Between black and white lie infinite levels of hue, reflections and silhouettes. As sunlight shifts and filters through leaves or curtains, levels of grey are constantly changing, ebbing and flowing as each shade fills with a new version of the colour before. Shadows and silhouettes can be used as decorative room elements so consider the direction the light is coming from.

Greenish tints of pale grey span thistle to sage, celadon to lichen. Darker shades include olive, khaki and slate. These softly-tinged green-greys provide wonderful backdrops in the home, offering a natural warmth while at the same time feeling peaceful and neutral. These are laid-back, placid shades, effortlessly surrounding us with a casual, unfussy sense of quiet style.

Left and above: Shadow and light play tricks with colour. Neutral and calming levels of grey are lifted and enlivened through golden, peachy tints of sunlight. Shadows and patterns cast by trees and plants dance on cool surfaces. Opaque and transparent layers move and change throughout the hours of day.

Following pages: A theatrical charcoal-black backdrop sets the scene for a collection of treasures on a white mantelpiece in a charming palette of ceramic-white, tinted grey, caramel, brass and antique gold.

Left: A blackened wallpaper by Sanderson is animated by its gold-printed bird motif. Pops of colour sing out against the dark background.

Right: Take inspiration from a favourite artwork when designing your colour scheme. Here, the dusted rose, peachy pink and warm olive shades from a painting are mirrored in the carefully chosen books and treasured possessions on the mantelpiece below.

Charcoal is a warmer alternative to true black. Choose a deep grey that holds nuances of either deep, dark brown or darkest forest. Pure jet black is often too stark and cold, but shades of ebony or nightshade offer a more 'coloured' super-dark effect. Accents of elderberry, wine and dusky rose spring to life when framed in dark charcoal. Play with paint samples and accessories to find the right charcoal hue for your space, ensuring it will complement your planned colour accents.

Use dark surfaces, the colours of a raven's wing or a heavy graphite shade, to pick out a piece of furniture or an architectural feature within a room. Focus on a chimney breast, fire surround, or mantelpiece in the deepest of colours to draw the eye. Contrast this with paler shades of dove or oyster grey on the remaining walls, to bring light into the room.

For plush, feather-filled velvet sofas and oversized lounge chairs deep stormy greys are an excellent choice. This enduring, timeless palette of greys can be easily updated and changed at whim, with the addition of a generous mix of cushions and other accessories. Deep ochre yellow and rich lagoon blues offer the perfect accent colours against grey.

Deep shades of darkest greys and blacks are perfect for display areas featuring treasured items, curios and other collections of objects. A dark backdrop has a dramatic effect on the bright coloured objects in the foreground. This 'cabinet of curiosities' effect is timeless, and creates a staged 'theatre' for your carefully curated personal belongings that tell your story.

Left and above: Curate a collection of objects with colours that tie into your chosen palette. Here, electric blue is picked out in the ornaments and the artworks. An unused fireplace can be filled with a collection of vintage glass baubles and trinkets, the light picking out jewel-like tones against the saturated black backdrop.

"Nature is painting for us, day after day, pictures of infinite beauty if only we have the eyes to see them." John Ruskin

STRING TO CHOCOLATE

NATURAL

———

Natural colours are undyed, unprocessed and uniquely imperfect. These are simple colours from wool to willow, tree bark to beach pebble, shades infused with honesty and warmth. They form the palette of humble objects that cry out to be touched, ones with finishes that are tactile, unpolished, fluffy and soft, or rugged and coarse. These are surfaces that affect and enhance the neutral nuances. Natural colours can be subtle and tinted like string, sand, buff or biscuit, or deep and evocative like nutmeg, tobacco, espresso and chocolate.

We look to surround ourselves with all things natural, seeking simplicity in a complex world. It is vital for humans to connect with natural elements and to experience the tactile pleasure of pebbles worn smooth by the sea, or wood that is mellowed by time, and natural fibres that are soft to touch and wear. This chapter celebrates the colours of materials such as clay or plaster, hemp cloth, linen and cotton, either undyed or coloured with plant-based pigments. Using the dye from roots, berries, bark, leaves generates soft, blurred tints. So choose these gentle colours and create a haven of tranquillity in your own home.

Embracing the natural palette puts emphasis on 'flawed' finishes too: edges may be frayed or surfaces unpolished, paintwork shows texture and brush marks, metals are naturally rusted. Nothing here is too perfect, we are celebrating the natural imperfections in everyday objects.

Above: This artist's home is filled with hand-painted surfaces and organic colours, inspired by the countryside where she lives.

Right: A glass and stone corridor links a renovated farmer's cottage to an architecturally designed barn conversion, cleverly combining new materials with old, natural with man-made.

Following pages: This vast kitchen and dining area celebrates natural materials and colours. Oak beams imbue warmth and the stone flooring beautifully contrasts pale oyster paintwork.

Natural colours, textures and uneven finishes contrast beautifully with modern glossy surfaces. Rustic touches of stone and bare or distressed wood give a homely, comforting feel to a space, but need to be offset with clean, more contemporary lines to prevent a space from becoming overly textural. Focus the interest into a specific space – a single wall or the front of a cabinet.

Wood is one of the earliest building materials. For millennia people have been using timber to craft their abodes, whether temporary frameworks covered with hides or thatch, or more permanent structures infilled with mud and straw. Abundant, strong, versatile and durable, wood is also beautiful. We want it for its natural colours and finish – from the palest, delicate Nordic birch and the golds and browns of beech and oak to the darkest ebony from Africa and Asia. Wonderfully worked to reveal its pattern, grain and texture, bare wood is as enduring as it is familiar in our homes. As a simple planked table, exposed beams and floorboards, or crafted into unique items of furniture that become part of the fabric of our lives, wood develops warm hues and character with age.

There is a thought that comfort is found in the way that things feel, rather than the way that things look. Modern homes are so often designed around how they look at the expense of how they feel. The aesthetic should not be at the expense of the tactile. When we love the feel as well as the look of our surroundings, we know we are at home, and we can truly relax and unwind.

Left and above: Wood which has aged over time develops a natural quality, which could never be mass produced. An antique shop cabinet is transformed into a beautiful and authentic kitchen island. Planked oak floorboards only improve with age, as the wear and tear of human activity slowly builds a unique patina and colour.

Left: Sun streams through the doorway of a mountain *finca* in southern Spain, highlighting the natural surfaces from terracotta floor tiles, to rustic wooden doors and an African embroidered leather seat.

Right: Pattern and decoration are created and formed through the fabric and construction of items within a home. Natural colour palettes and geometric shapes emerge within the beautifully tactile wool cushions, cane furniture and basketware.

The joy of decorating with a natural palette is that all the tones and nuances work so beautifully together. Taking our cue from nature, we can contrast the velvety greys and browns seen in a moth's wing or the peeling bark of weathered timber with the warm creamy tones of canvas, faded natural plaster or pale, porcelain-like seashells.

Layer upon layer of surface and texture happily blend within this gentle set of colours. The warm hues of

different types of wood introduce their wonderfully unique colour into a scheme. They serve as strong foundations on which to build, perhaps adding a flash of colour, such as the bright ochre yellow in the handle of the basket or the earthy, spiced red stripes seen in the cushions here. Keep your highlight colours within the natural spectrum, using autumnal yellows and oranges, or orange-hued reds and terracottas, to complement the natural browns within a scheme.

Colour does not always have to be applied to a room or a scheme. We can opt for building materials that provide the perfect natural hue. Allow one wall within a kitchen, bathroom or living room to be hewn from exposed rock or natural red brick. Ceilings are too often neglected in a decorating scheme, but exposed rafters and ceiling tiles will bring richness and interest to a natural scheme.

Blocks of colour break up a neutral scheme that could otherwise seem too flat or cool. Earthy reddish browns – umber, sienna and terracotta – add an instant welcoming note to offset the pale hues. If you are decorating within an existing space, cladding is a wonderful material to consider. You can source reclaimed finishes for an instantly aged and 'lived-in' feel; old tiles or salvaged timbers lend

a sense of permanence. Wood panelling and veneers add an instant hit of warmth to a space. Be adventurous and consider different ways of incorporating wood: floorboards on walls or cladding on a ceiling, for example. Always balance the matt and rustic finishes with an accent of metal or glass: copper, rose gold or brass light fittings and accessories will bring their warm glow to a space.

Left and above: Natural colours and materials flow easily from interior to exterior living spaces, whether your home is a city apartment or a house facing the sea on the Greek island of Ithaca. An element of contrast within a neutral scheme will evoke an elegant, well-considered finish.

NATURAL: STRING TO CHOCOLATE

Your bedroom needs to be a sanctuary. Use materials that make you feel instantly cosy and cocooned – soft blankets and throws made from wool, cashmere and mohair, faux fur or velvet to delight the skin. Deep moody shades of tobacco, toast and coffee are restorative and welcoming here. Add a touch of decadence with metallic gold surfaces, which reflect and catch the atmospheric lighting.

Left and above: Every surface is considered in these sumptuous bedrooms – even the ceiling is decorated. Pattern and texture delight the senses and play with a rich palette of deep toasted browns. Accents and highlights appear through gold and lustrous finishes, here foiled leather, sequins and reflective glass.

"White…is not a mere absence of colour; it is a shining and affirmative thing, as fierce as red, as definite as black…God paints in many colours; but He never paints so gorgeously, as when He paints in white." G. K. Chesterton

PAPER TO SNOW

WHITE

———

White is a blank page upon which to begin. White is innocent, untouched, uncontaminated and true. We associate white with morning time, when everything is light and fresh, a new dawn and a new beginning. Clean white bed sheets, crisp white pyjamas, a jug of fresh milk. A pure white home can feel too clinical, too sterile to some. Yet to others, a light-filled whitened room is the perfect retreat; a heavenly, illuminated, meditative space. White elevates the everyday and shines her light on everything around her, dazzling us with her simple, pure beauty.

Like no other colour white enhances the sense of space. It is filled with light and brightens any area in which it is used – two qualities many people welcome in their homes. White is therefore often seen as the safest option. However, because the brightest pure white reflects light it can be dazzling in direct sunlight. It can also make a room feel cold or even harsh and clinical, unless accented with a good dose of hot, bright colour. Gentle hues of off-whites soften the effects of light, giving a more diffused finish.

Layer subtle shades of white and tinted white, from parchment to chalk, sugar white to goose feather. Use textures and contrasting materials to bring such a sparse palette to life. Mix ecru or bleached linen with off-white cowhide, and sketched paper whites with matt whitewashed walls. All woodwork can be painted with a matt chalky finish; choose greyish tints of white like feather for window frames and items of furniture. Artwork will also add interest to an otherwise 'colourless' scheme.

Of course, we refer to 'white' but nothing on these pages is truly white. These timeless monochromatic colour schemes combine off-whites with near blacks, and the subtle tinted colours are more gentle on the eye. Unfussy, effortless and timeless, this classic colour palette will out-live every future colour trend. Off-white is more natural, softer and more flattering shade, instantly sophisticated and elegant in its modesty, with a mellow warm glow. Select the warmer tones of white, ranging from pinkish tinted whites – 'piglet' white is an all-time favourite – to linen, shirting, paper or porcelain. And the 'black' here is dark ebony, a warmish shade of super black-brown, or charcoal grey or even very inky forest green. The almost-black colours are less harsh than pure black, softer and easier to work with.

Any seeming absence of colour within these images requires closer attention. The different surfaces and finishes here reveal the infinite subtle variations in tone. Whitened schemes, therefore, require just as much thought as a brightly coloured space. Incorporating pattern and decoration into these simplistic schemes shows that whites are anything but boring.

Left and above: Bring unexpected pattern and decoration into the details within your home. From a painted archway in the Amber Fort in Jaipur, India, to hand-painted ceramic plates in South Africa, simple graphic illustration is refined and timeless.

Greyish whites with a chalky finish feel as though they have existed forever. Look for finishes that suggest something aged, weathered and crumbling. Colours and surfaces that could tell a story and colours filled with wistful memories will add layers of emotion to a space. A classic combination to consider is whites and faded summer blues. Bleached summer skies, Mediterranean painted doorways and the wash of the clear blue ocean over sea-worn pebbles can all inspire a room scheme.

Blueish, greenish colours, somewhere between duck-egg and seafoam will lift an otherwise white scheme. Try adding textiles in either faded turquoise or softened aqua as a secondary colour. Texture adds depth and interest to a pale colour scheme. Play with contrasting materials and notice how soft, matt surfaces, such as natural fabrics, absorb the light and clean bright white expanses bounce the light around and create the illusion of more space.

WHITE: PAPER TO SNOW

Gently tinted, milky-hued white walls will never tire with age. These clean and timeless colours, will remain relevant and modern regardless of trend and fashion. In design, white and off-white colour palettes have long since been associated with elegance, and a high-end aesthetic. Whites can be used in any style or era of building. Furniture and art stand out against a white background, a wooden floor will glow when contrasted with clean white walls.

Warmer, tinted, natural whites have a ceramic, chalky feel; they evoke a softened, gentle environment. It is beautiful to layer white tones, and natural cream or stone together, there are no rules, use every shade of white on different textures and surfaces.

White is a powerful colour, it acts as an instant cleanser, a dynamic purifying element which will transform any room. Painting a wall white is like an instant spring-clean, creating a perfect, uncluttered and vibrant atmosphere.

Left and right: Use white stoneware and ceramics in the kitchen and the bathroom, from stone mosaic walls, to marble or quartz worktops. Untreated bare whitened plaster walls, white ceramic basins, and enamel bathtubs all have a feel of luxury. Porcelain glaze, earthenware and china tableware, or a clay bead lampshade all offer nuances and tints of whites.

Pure white interiors are given a touch of homeliness and comfort through the addition of natural materials and natural accent colours. A whitewashed room needs to be softened and becomes instantly inviting through the use of warm mid-tone browns. Brown with white is a refreshing alternative to black and white, and one that is just as elegant.

Darker brown colours from leather upholstery or polished natural wood add contrast. Tones of coffee, peppercorn, or bitter chocolate can be used throughout a scheme, from dark wooden floorboards, to cowhide-covered furniture, or ancient wooden carvings. Raw materials such as wood, wicker, leather and stone all have an earthy coloration. Soft and buttery tones of biscuit,

caramel, sand and string have a golden quality, like sunlight filtering through the window, instantly warming the white walls. Natural bamboo, hemp or seagrass matting for the floor, woven baskets filled with stacks of natural linen cushions and even piles of vintage books with yellowing pages – all add warmth and a sense of comfort to a room scheme.

Left and above: Interior and exterior spaces with whitewashed walls contrast beautifully together with natural surfaces and colours. Earthy browns offer a never-ending palette of tonal shades to play with against your white backdrop. A nomadic collection of accessories, cushions, fabrics and rugs are sourced from around the world, imposing a comfortable, bohemian vibe.

This palette of whites and blues is as uplifting and invigorating as an early morning swim. Immersive depths of blues and aquas, reflect against the clear white shades, these are key shades for textiles and accessories in the bathroom and the kitchen.

Mix differing levels of blues and greens, colours like the ocean, ever-changing blues from cobalt and ultramarine through to deep cyan. Bright swimming-pool blues and fresh turquoise colours are inspired by exotic destinations and island life. Outdoor living is mainly reserved for hotter climates, places with endless days of sunshine and lack of rain, but wherever you live, take inspiration from this sun-drenched lifestyle. We can pour a little holiday colour into our own homes, and evoke a sense of escape.

Left and right: Energizing and uplifting, these refreshing, radiant whites and clear, shimmering blues reflect the light and enhance a cooling and serene atmosphere.

Following pages: From this decorated lounge area we can see that white is anything but simple or stark. Layers of painterly texture, fabric interest and lime-washed wood evoke a serene yet inviting space. Touches and accents of deep indigo blue and rose pink enliven the scheme, turning it from pale and pastel, to alive and vibrant.

Oyster to alabaster, limestone to sail cloth, nothing here is truly white. Nature often provides us with the most perfect of colours, where nothing needs to be altered or improved upon. You could create an entire colour scheme from a single seashell, its palette ranging from pinkish white, to tinted, cosmetic peach, to powder blush, vanilla tinged, skin pink or nude. These are gentle and barely there colours, a hint of colour upon white, a mere trace of a shade. Every room in the house can be decorated with this authentic blend of non-colours, shades and nuances of white, cream, eggshell, and everything in-between. Then layer accents and hues in contrasting shades in order to define areas and build interest, from natural linen and stone, to pale tints of blues or pinks.

Surface interest adds depth to colour combinations, from natural stoneware tiles, crackle glaze finishes and unpainted plaster walls. Soft and hard surfaces are combined, building light and shade throughout. Layers of whites evoke a feeling of tranquillity and luxury, like a secret sanctuary in your own home, the atmosphere of a spa, filled with tactile surfaces and luxurious scents.

Left and above: Collect vintage and hand-crafted ceramic ware to inspire subtle colour palettes, from pale cloud and glazed whites, to tinted sugar or lily whites. Translucent and opaque glass, washed and weathered wood and dip-dyed linen offer evocative and intriguing surfaces for these pale and faded shades.

Left and above: Graphic illustrations and colour-filled patterns are simplistic and fun. Pure daubs of strong colours are surrounded by white, and elements within the scheme are framed with a fine black line, giving a refined, graphic finish.

A white wall is like an empty gallery waiting to be filled. Have fun and add splashes of colour and accents through playful accessories and artwork. Mix and match printed textiles or collections of colourful books to create pops of colour. A pop of marmalade orange, a flash of brilliant green, or a highlight of cobalt blue, draws the eye without overpowering your white scheme.

RESOURCES

ADDRESS BOOK

Designers, architects and makers of products, designs and artworks that appear in the book are listed here. (For the restaurants, hotels, guesthouses, museums and galleries that feature, see page 253.)

ARCHITECTS, ARTISTS & PHOTOGRAPHERS

Gecko Designs, Málaga, Spain (pages 240, 245)
www.geckodisenos.weebly.com

Johanna Halford (fruit still lifes, pages 43 and 61)
www.johannahalford.net

Guy Holloway Architects, London and Hythe, Kent, UK (page 194)
www.guyholloway.co.uk

Adrian Johnson (print, *Basilicas*, page 92 (left))
www.adrianjohnsonstudio.com

Jeffrey Kroll (painting, page 41)
www.krollogy.com

Chris Levine (painting *Equanimous 1*, pages 218–19)
www.chrislevine.com

Casey Moore (photographs of the author, page 9)
www.caseymoore.com

Patrick Thomas (artwork *Shot Heart/Target Fluoro Red*, page 86)
www.patrickthomas.com

Kristjana S. Williams (artwork page 210 (left))
www.kristjanaswilliams.com

Jessica Zoob (pages 21 (top), 215, 216, 234 (centre left, centre right, btm left), 237 (btm), 242–3, 244 (left))
www.jessicazoob.com

INTERIOR DESIGNERS, WALLPAPER & FABRIC MANUFACTURERS

Black Parrots Studio (pages featuring interior and wallpaper designs: 26 (btm), 80–1, 128, 223 (top right); pages featuring interior design only: 34, 58, 62, 75, 109 (left), 122, 139, 180, 227, 247 (left))
Interior design and products including wallpaper, fabric, cushions and lighting
www.blackparrotsstudio.com

Chhatwal & Jonsson (cushions 'Kulgam' page 120 (left))
Swedish home textiles brand created by Stig Jonsson and Geetali Chhatwal Jonsson
www.chhatwal-jonsson.se

Christina Lundsteen (cushions 'Blair' page 146)
Danish designer of luxury, handmade cushions with Europe-wide stockists
www.christinalundsteen.com

Cole & Son (pages 145, 150, 160, 170)
Manufacturers of fine printed wallpapers and interior fabrics in the UK since 1875, offering both classic and beautiful contemporary designs
www.cole-and-son.com

Designers Guild (pink chair fabric pages 33 and 147; swatches 179)
UK-based homeware, paint and textiles brand synonymous with colour and vibrant pattern
www.designersguild.com

Anna Hayman (pages 23, 38, 70 (btm left), 82 (right), 111 (fabric by Biba), 112 (left), 114 (top right), 226)
UK-based luxury print designer creating wallpaper, lampshades, cushions and fabrics
www.annahaymandesigns.com

House of Hackney (cushions page 82)
Modern design label focused on British-made goods offering dramatic original prints across homewares and clothing online and from the flagship store in London
www.houseofhackney.com

Jake Phipps (lamps 'Jeeves & Wooster' page 247 (left))
British furniture and lighting designer
www.jakephipps.com

Judeco (wall lamp 'Couronne' and mirror 'Corona Sun' page 168 (right))
Makers of luminaires, furniture, upholstery and decoration based in Herent, Belgium
www.judeco.be

Lapuan Kankurit, Oy (blankets 'Corona' and 'Kaarna', designed by Marja Rautiainen, woven by Lapuan Kankurit, page 50 (btm left))
Fourth-generation weavers with a store and studio in Helsinki, Finland
www.lapuankankurit.fi

Mink Interiors (cushion stockist, cover and page 146)
Retail store, interior design studio and webshop based in Kent, UK
www.minkinteriors.com

Noam Dover and Michal Cederbaum ('Tailormade Vases', page 214 (top left))
Israeli-based designers of one-off textile and art pieces
www.noamandmichal.com

Playroom Interiors (pages 36 (left), 135, 247 (right))
Range of British wallpapers and accessories for children's spaces by Emma Carlow
www.playroominteriors.com

Romo Ltd (fabrics page 12, 15, 179)
British interior brand specializing in fabrics, wall coverings and accessories
www.romo.com

Sanderson (wallpaper page 208 (right))
The oldest manufacturer of soft furnishings in the UK, now offering wallpaper, fabrics and paint
www.stylelibrary.com/sanderson

Svenskt Tenn ('Elephant' wallpaper, by Estrid Ericsson, pages 72 (left), 203)
Swedish interior design studio, store and online services
www.svenskttenn.se

Temper Studio + Anna Glover Interiors (Anna Glover wallpaper and SPAN daybed page 59 (right))
Contemporary hand-made furniture and household objects from a studio in Wiltshire, UK
www.temperstudio.com

Timorous Beasties (wallpaper page 125)
Scottish design team noted for surreal and provocative textiles and wallpapers
www.timorousbeasties.com

PAINT MANUFACTURERS

Bauwerk Paint (shade cards page 12; also pages 20, 221)
www.bauwerkcolour.com

Earthborn (pages 97 (right), 199, 201)
www.earthbornpaints.com

Farrow & Ball (pages 12, 17, 22, 48, 60, 89, 124, 127, 199, 201)
www.farrow-ball.com

Little Greene Paint Company (cover image; also pages 6, 8, 13, 17, 113, 146–7, 172)
www.littlegreene.com

TILES & CERAMICS
Bert and May (page 202 (right))
Modern tiles and accessories designed in the UK and made in Europe
www.bertandmay.com

Bloomingville (page 179)
Global brand, rooted in the Danish aesthetic tradition for interior design and homeware
www.bloomingville.com

Emery et Cie (pages 37, 48 (right), 89, 93, 205 (left))
Belgian homeware brand based in Antwerp offering artisan produced tiles, fabrics
and paints, with a deep and saturated colour palette
www.emeryetcie.com

Christiane Perrochon, Atelia di Ceramica (page 156 (right))
Swiss ceramicist based in Tuscany, Italy, with the most beautiful eye for colour
www.christianeperrochon.com

Sue Pryke (page 197 (right))
UK-based ceramicist making contemporary hand made ceramics and tableware
www.suepryke.com

Topsy Jewell Pottery (page 195 (centre left))
Potter based in Sussex, UK, making hand-thrown pots in white stoneware clay
www.topsyjewell.com

HOMEWARE & ACCESSORIES
A Modern Grand Tour (page 157 (left))
A carefully curated collection of antique furniture and interior objects housed in
an English stately home, Aynhoe Park, Oxfordshire, UK
www.amoderngrandtour.com

Anthropologie (tieback page 72 (left); towel page 150)
A global collection of clothing and homewares
www.anthropologie.com

Argent & Sable Designs (page 129 (btm))
Makers of vintage signs and vintage fairground-inspired lights
www.argentandsabledesigns.co.uk

Bethan Gray (pages 66 (centre right), 154 (centre right))
London-based luxury furniture designer
www.bethangray.com

Caro Somerset (pages 84–5, 152–3, 200, 202 (left), 204 (right))
One-off lifestyle boutique in a charming village in Somerset, UK
www.carosomerset.com

Design Afrika (woven bag, page 223)
Cape Town-based company that designs and promotes ethically crafted hand-
woven basketry and fabrics
www.designafrika.co.za

Ferm Living (laundry bag, page 201)
Scandinavian homewares brand with a touch of mid-century charm
www.fermliving.com

Flint (pages 188 (right); wall hanging 210 (right))
Boutique in Sussex, UK, stocking homewares, books, fashion and flowers
www.flintcollection.com

From Victoria (plates page 15; linen page 20)
Boutique in Sussex, UK, selling homewares, books and indoor plants
www.fromvictoria.co.uk

i gigi (page 214 (top centre))
Café/homeware store in Sussex, UK, selling a carefully curated collection of natural
and neutral ceramics and furniture
www.igigigeneralstore.com

IKEA (cushions page 103 (right))
Iconic global brand with affordable, fun textiles and accessories
www.ikea.co.uk

Kent & London (pages 114 (btm left), 225 (left))
Designers/makers of furniture, kitchens, interiors with bases in Kent and London, UK
www.kentandlondon.co.uk

Made (bedlinen page 20)
Online-only homeware brand working directly with the makers, offering affordable
furniture and textiles
www.made.com

Munna and Ginger & Jagger (pages 129 (top), 181 (top))
Portugal-based designers of hand-crafted, contemporary products inspired by nature
www.gingerandjagger.com

Merci (page 50 (btm centre))
Paris café/clothing store and a quirky mix of branded and own-brand home accessories
www.merci-merci.com

Objet de Curiosité (pages 157 (right), 181 (btm), 211 (left))
Shop in the Rhône, France, offering unique pieces from the natural world, from
crystals to butterfly domes, stuffed birds to seashells
www.objetdecuriosite.com

Popsicle (pages 88, 108)
Boutique in Sussex, UK, filled with colourful home accessories and clothing
www.popsicleonline.com

Rock the Kasbah by Philippe Xerri (page 233 (left))
Urban-ethnic inspired design brand with showrooms in France and Tunisia
www.rockthekasbah.net

Toast (bedlinen page 20)
Online fashion and interior brand, with a natural sensibility
www.toast.com

FASHION
Dries Van Noten (shoe, page 6, top centre)
Belgian fashion designer and luxury brand
www.driesvannoten.be

Etro (skirt pages 6 (top right), 83 (left))
Italian fashion house headquartered in Milan
www.etro.com

Maison Margiela (knitware pages 6 (top right), 83 (left))
Belgian fashion house headquartered in Paris
www.maisonmargiela.com/gb

LOCATIONS

———

Included here are locations photographed for the book that are accessible to the public, together with details of the interiors industry trade fairs, showcasing designers' and manufacturers' work.

PUBLIC SPACES, RESTAURANTS, CAFES & PLACES TO STAY

10 Corso Como, Milan, Italy (page 232 (right))
Beautifully curated boutique and restaurant
www.10corsocomo.com/location-milano

Amber Fort, Jaipur, India (pages 183, 232 left))

Anokhi Museum of Hand Printing, Amber, Jaipur, India (page 113 (right))
Museum and workshop showcasing block printed fabrics
www.anokhi.com/museum

Archangel, Frome, Somerset, UK (page 189 (left))
A restored former coaching inn, now hotel and restaurant
www.archangelfrome.com

Bell Inn, Ticehurst, Kent, UK (page 126 (left))
A quirky hotel and restaurant with fun interior design
www.thebellinticehurst.com

Caravane Boutique, Tarifa, Cadiz, Spain (pages 72 (right), 73 (left), 103 (left), 134 (btm centre))
Lifestyle boutique in southern Spain
www.tarifaweb.com

Casa de La Luz, Andalucia, Spain (pages 103 (right), 112 (right), 222, 238)
Mountain *finca* designed and built by Anna Starmer and husband Iain
www.casadelaluz.weebly.com

Casa Las Tortugas, Isla Holbox, Mexico (page 241 (btm))
Beachside spa and hotel on a tiny island in the Mexican Caribbean
www.holboxcasalastortugas.com

Casa No. 6, Centro Cultural, Campeche, Mexico (pages 95, 100, 101)
Renovated mansion house and living museum
www.campeche.travel/centro-cultural-casa-no-6

Casa Susegad, Goa, India (pages 25, 53 (left), 102 (left) 141 (left))
Restored mansion house in the foothills of the Western Ghats, now a hotel
www.casasusegad.com

City Palace, Jaipur, India (page 114 (centre left))
Palace complex in Jaipur, the capital of Rajasthan

Cortijo El Carligto, Málaga, Spain (pages 224 (left), 238 (right))
Luxury *fincas* in the heart of Andalucia, for high-end holidays and travel experiences
www.carligto.com

Dar Azaouia, Asilah, Morocco (page 231)
Guesthouse in a converted home in the medina
www.darazaouia-asilah.com

Hauser & Wirth, Durslade Farmhouse, Somerset, UK (pages 27, 49, 56, 74, 104–5, 136–7, 141 (right), 142, 170, 187, 196 (left), 216 (right))
Gallery and multi-purpose arts centre, one of eight locations of Hauser & Wirth, the international gallery devoted to contemporary art and modern masters. (Renovation and interior design of Durslade: Luis Laplace)
www.hauserwirthsomerset.com

House in Hastings, Sussex, UK (pages 28 (left), 31, 54–5, 57, 63, 73, 76, 78–9, 144)
A colour-filled house by the sea for parties and weekend getaways
www.houseinhastings.co.uk

Itha 108, Ithaca, Greece (pages 225 (right), 234 (top left))
Yoga centre and retreat on the idyllic Greek island of Ithaca
www.itha108.com

Le Jardin des Biehn, Fez, Morocco (pages 1, 30 (right), 47, 48, 51, 53 (right), 67, 102, 236)
Riad, hotel and café in the heart of the medina
www.jardindesbiehn.com

No Vacancy Kadikoy, Istanbul, Turkey (page 70 (top left))
Boutique gift store
+90 531 286 9427

Palacio do Deão, Quepem, Goa, India (pages 6, 158, 241 (right))
A restored Portuguese mansion house in Goa
www.palaciododeao.com

Petersham Nurseries, Richmond, Surrey, UK (page 237 (top))
Michelin-starred café and lifestyle store on the outskirts of London
www.petershamnurseries.com

Posada Margherita, Tulum, Yucatan, Mexico (pages 69, 245)
Hotel and Italian restaurant
www.posadamargherita.com

Prospect Cottage, Dungeness, Kent, UK (page 94 (top right))
The former home and garden of film maker Derek Jarman

Rosas & Xocolate, Mérida, Yucatan, Mexico (pages 148, 162, 164–5)
Boutique hotel and spa
www.rosasandxocolate.com

Safari, Tulum, Yucatan, Mexico (page 70 (btm right))
Beachside restaurant
www.safaritulum.com.mx

Sanará, Tulum, Yucatan, Mexico (page 235)
Yoga centre with beach-front bungalows
www.sanaratulum.com

Sketch, Mayfair, London, UK (page 83 (right))
Renowned restaurant and tea shop (featured design: Carolyn Quartermaine)
www.sketch.london

Riad Lolita, Costa de La Luz, Jerez, Spain (pages 39 (top), 46 (right), 198)
A historic merchant's house at the southernmost tip of Europe
www.tarifabeachhouses.com

Villas HM Palapas del Mar, Isla Holbox, Mexico (page 71)
Beach bungalows and restaurant on a tiny island off the coast of Mexico
www.hmhotels.net

TRADE FAIRS

100% Design Exhibition, London (page 50 (top left))
Professional trade fair dedicated to interior design and architecture
www.100percentdesign.co.uk

Maison & Objet, Paris, France (pages 26 (top), 35 (top))
Professional trade fair dedicated to lifestyle, decoration and design
www.maison-objet.com

INDEX

A

accent colours 42, 43, 57, 66
  green 70
  grey 200, 208, 210
  natural colours 222
  orange 109, 115, 120, 125
  pink 168
  purple 178, 181
  red 138, 141, 143, 144
  and surface finishes 63
  white 230, 247
  yellow 89, 92, 95–6, 99
accent lighting 39
Africa 59, 102, 103, 113, 220, 233
  (see also Morocco)
Amber (Amer) Fort 182, 230
ambient lighting 39
architectural features 40–1, 109
Asia *see* India, Turkey, Vietnam

B

Barragán, Luis 163
bathrooms 21, 26, 28, 135
  blue 47
  grey 192
  natural colours 212, 224
  orange 112, 124
  pink 150–1
  white 237, 241
bedrooms 19, 20, 24, 28, 36
  black 23
  cool colours 28–9
  green 74–5
  natural colours 226–7
  orange 110
  pink 151, 170
  purple 178
  yellow 97
black 23
  contrast colour 33
  and white 33, 70, 72, 92, 125,
    199, 202–4, 232
  with yellow 103
blends 35
blue 12–13, 16–17, 42–3, 44–63
  cool colours 28
  dark colours 22
  emotion 19
  with green 79
  with orange 52–3, 58, 115
  with red 60, 63
  with white 51, 58, 235, 240–1
  with white and red 135
  with yellow 90–3, 99
breakfast rooms 143
bright colours 24–5, 33, 138–9, 166
brown 238

C

calming colours 20–1, 46, 67
charcoal 33, 72–3, 92, 125, 173,
  199, 202, 206–8, 232
  chitose midori 85
circadian rhythm 39
City Palace, Rajasthan, India 114
cladding 224–5
clashing colours 21, 25, 146, 166–7
colour zones 25, 122
complementary colours 24, 42, 53,
  122, 181
contrast colour 25, 32–3, 35, 36,
  40, 42, 48
  blue 58, 60, 63
  orange 110, 122
  pink 161, 166
  red 141, 144
  yellow 99, 103
cool colours 25, 28–9, 46, 67
  contrast colour 33
  orange 110

D

dark colours 22–3
  and small spaces 22, 60
daylight 39, 46, 104, 159, 196, 230
  time of day 16, 39, 159, 197
  see also light
Denmark 116, 117
dining rooms 22
  blue 60
  natural colours 218–19
  pink 168
  purple 181
  red 143, 144

E

emotion 19, 24
  orange 109
  purple 178
  red 131
  yellow 87, 89, 95, 97, 99, 101, 104
entrance halls 15, 25
  grey 198–9, 203
  red 136–7
  yellow 95

F

fabrics
  bright colours 24
  cool colours 28
  dark colours 22
  green 71, 76
  natural colours 223, 227

orange 110, 122–3, 126–7
pink 155, 157, 171, 173
purple 179, 187, 189
warm colours 26
white 230, 235
yellow 92–3, 103
'flawed' finishes 215

G

gold 39, 93, 226–7
Greece 225, 235
green 30–1, 64–85
  with blue 79
  emotion 19
  with grey 205
  with pink 160–1, 166–7
  with purple 182–5
  with red 70, 71, 132–3
  with white 235
grey 20–1, 190–211
  with green 205
  with orange 125
  with pink 152–3
  with yellow 92, 103

H

Holi festival 166–7
hot colours 60, 116
hue 30–1, 133, 140

I

Ibiza 46–7
Iceland 109
India 25, 30, 32, 52–3, 102, 113,
  114, 115, 161, 166–7, 171, 182,
  230, 233
indigo 59
inspiration 10–13
Italy 156–7

K

keepsakes 58, 138–9, 211
kitchens
  green 68
  lighting in 39
  natural colours 218–19, 221, 224
  orange 109, 112
  pink 163
  purple 178
  white 241
  yellow 19, 98–9

L

light 16, 38–9
cool colours 22, 28
  mood effects 19
  pink 159
  shadows 204–5
  and surface finishes 63
  warm colours 26
  white 230
  see also daylight; lighting
lighting 19, 26, 39, 60, 227
  green 76, 83, 85
  grey 196
  orange 115, 128–9
  pink 157
  purple 189
  red 141
living rooms 19, 33
  blue 60
  green 75
  natural colours 224
  orange 110
  pink 163, 168
  purple 181
  red 146–7
  white 242–3
  yellow 92

M

matt finish 35, 51
  green 85
  orange 110
  purple 189
  white 235
Mexico 71, 89, 95, 100–1, 116,
  132–3, 162–3, 235
Morocco 32, 36, 51, 103, 114, 230
metals 121, 193, 225
mood *see* emotion
mood boards 10, 11, 13, 14

N

natural colours 212–27, 237–9, 244
natural materials 71, 120, 238–9
  grey 194–5
  with orange 125
  with pink 159
  nature 67–8
  green 83
  natural colours 222
  pink 164–5
  purple 181–5
  white 244
  neutral tints 21

CREDITS

All photographs in this book are taken by Anna Starmer with the exception of the portraits on page 9, which are reproduced with the kind permission of Casey Moore.

This book is presented solely for information purposes. The content and images in the book is the sole expression and opinion of its author, and not necessarily that of the publisher. No warranties or guarantees are expressed or implied by the publisher's choice to include any of the content in this volume. While best efforts have been used in preparing this book and acknowledging all the sources of the images, neither the author nor the publisher shall be liable for any physical, psychological, emotional, financial or commercial damages, including, but not limited to, special, incidental, consequential or other damages caused, or alleged to have been caused, directly or indirectly, by the information and images contained herein. The author and publishers wish to acknowledge and thank the following organizations and individuals whose property appears in this book.

Catherine Agnew/Riad Lolita Tarifa 39 (top), 46 (right), 198

Anokhi Museum/Rachel Bracken-Singh 113 (right)

Lisa Richardson 121 (left)

Archangel/Ross Nichol, Frome, Somerset, UK 189 (left)

Bell Inn, Ticehurst, Kent, UK 126 (left)

Bethan Gray 66 (centre right), 154 (centre right)

Black Parrots Studio/Alexa de Castilho and Sarah Mitchenall (see page 250)

Ellen Brookes 33 (top), 138 (right) 208, 233 (right)

Caravane Boutique 72 (right), 73 (left), 103 (left), 134 (btm centre)

Emma Carlow 36 (left), 92 (left), 97 (left), 98, 135, 247 (right)

Caro Somerset/Natalie Jones 84, 85, 152, 153, 200, 202 (left), 204 (right)

Casa Susegad/Norman and Carole Steen 25, 53 (left), 102 (left), 141 (left)

Casa Las Tortugas/Patrick Wiering 241 (btm)

Cortijo El Carligto/Alan Hazel and Marc Wils 224 (left), 238 (right)

Dar Azaouia/Caroline Vanthuyne 231

Dries Van Noten 6 (centre)

Ellie-Rose Warner 6 (top right), 83 (left) (skirt Etro, knitware Maison Margiela)

Flint/Heidi Francis 188 (right), 210 (right)

Gecko Disenos/James and Robert Richardson 240, 245 (right)

Hauser & Wirth Gallery/Durslade Farmhouse/Emily Ridler 27, 49, 56, 74 (artwork Phyllida Barlow, *Untitled: floodlights* © Phyllida Barlow Courtesy Phyllida Barlow and Hauser & Wirth), 104, 105, 136–7 (artwork Pipilotti Rist, *Untitled* (from the Basel Serie)/Serie J 1993/97, C-Print Videostill © Pipilotti Rist, Courtesy Pipilotti Rist and Hauser & Wirth), 141 (right), 142 (artwork André Thomkins, –Knopio © The Estate of André Thomkins Courtesy the Estate and Hauser & Wirth), 170 (artwork Pipilotti Rist, *Allergic Rose* 2007 Still life photo print on rag paper © Pipilotti Rist Courtesy Pipilotti Rist and Hauser & Wirth), 187 (left), 216 (right)

Anna Hayman 23 (artwork Anna Hayman), 38, 70 (btm left, artwork Anna Hayman), 82 (right), 111, 112 (left), 114 (top right), 226

Eva Hickinbottom 204 (left)

House in Hastings/Paul Brewster 28, 31, 54–5, 57 (right), 63, 73 (right), 76, 78, 79, 144

Itha 108/Ingrid Gottschalk 225 (right) 234 (top left)

Jardin des Biehn/Cafe Fez 1, 30 (right), 46 (left), 47, 48 (left), 51, 53 (right), 67, 102, 238

Topsy Jewell 195 (centre left)

Laupan Kankurit/Jaana Hjelt 50 (btm left)

Emily Mellor 36 (right), 72 (left), 77, 86 (artwork *Heart/Target #03* (Red) by Patrick Thomas), 92 (right), 145, 189 (right), 202 (right), 203, 206 (right), 206–7

Nicole Page-Croft 220 (left), 239 (left)

Popsicle/Sharon Makgill 88, 108

Posada Margherita/Alessandro Carozzino 69, 245 (left)

Rosas & Xocolate/Kolozs Carol Fischer 148, 162, 164–5

Ann Louise Roswald 22 (top), 37, 43 (still life fruit Johanna Halford), 60, 61, 124, 173

Lucy Russell 21 (btm), 22 (btm), 40, 44, 123, 192, 220 (right, artwork Marcus James), 221 (left)

Safari Restaurant 70 (btm right)

Anna Starmer/Sussex UK cover, 17, 33 (btm), 48 (right, 82 (left), 89, 96 (right), 97 (right) 126 (right), 127, 146, 147, 150, 151, 152 (left) 160, 168 (left), 172, 199 (top and btm), 201, 209, 210 (artwork Kristjana S. Williams), 211 (right), 213, 221

Anna Starmer/Casa de la Luz, Andalucia, Spain 103 (right) 112 (right), 113 (left), 222, 238 (Casa de La Luz, Jerez, Spain)

Sophie Stevenson 29, 39 (btm), 41 (painting, Jeffrey Kroll), 68 (left), 121 (right), 212, 217, 218–219 (painting *Equanimous 1*, Chris Levine, 2008 by kind permission of the artist), 246 (artworks (top) *Woman with Bow* and *Woman with Striped Skirt* by Joanna Ham, and (below) *Hitch* by Natasha Law, Courtesy of the artist and Eleven Fine Art)

Temper Studio/George Winks and Anna Glover 59 (right)

Timorous Beasties/Paul Simmons and Alistair McAuley 125

Sketch/Ellen Payne 83 (right)

Villas HM Palapas del Mar/Joan Ximenis 71

Kristjana S. Williams 210 (left, artwork)

Jessica Zoob 21 (top), 215, 216 (left), 234 (centre left, centre right, btm left), 237 (btm), 242–3, 244 (left)

This booklet contains colour swatches of my absolute favourite combinations and ideas from *Love Colour*. Its purpose is to provide a curated selection of colours that are practical and timeless as well as beautiful.

There are ten groups of colours, following the chapter colour themes. Within each group I have collated pale and light tints, mid tones and deep dark shades that will inspire and delight. The colours are arranged with regard to their hue and tone to make it easier to match complementary or contrasting and accent colours. For instance, in blues you will find those with a green cast, such as duck egg or aqua, placed opposite more violet-tinted ones, such as sky blue and deep indigo.

Use this booklet for planning and designing your own schemes. Make notes on it to highlight the colours you really love. Fold back the pages to match the swatches to your favourite fabric or an object you truly treasure. Take it with you when you are sourcing materials or furniture and accessories. Ask your paint supplier to make up the closest match to your chosen key shades and in the finish you are looking for.

For the home decorator it is a joy to find the right shade that exactly matches what you have in mind. I hope you will carry this handy booklet as a quick reference guide to inspire colour schemes and spark new ideas for years to come.

Anna Starmer

BLUE Sky to Indigo

p.48

p.48

p.53

p.47

p.51

p.53

p.45

p.53

p.51

p.46

p.48

p.57

p.59

p.47

p.62

p.60

GREEN
Pistachio to Forest

p.75

p.75

p.76

p.72

p.78

p.73

p.73

p.82

p.72

p.68

p.68

p.75

p.64

p.76

p.83

p.85

YELLOW

Buttercup to Turmeric

p.99

p.95

p.95

p.89

p.89

p.104

p.92

p.89

p.95

p.93

p.101

p.99

p.101

p.102

p.94

p.104

ORANGE Apricot to Copper

p.121

p.120

p.126

p.113

p.108

p.110

p.112

p.115

p.116

p.107

p.126

p.122

p.108

p.126

p.129

p.129

RED Scarlet to Ruby

p.138

p.141

p.146

p.133

p.131

p.143

p.140

p.140

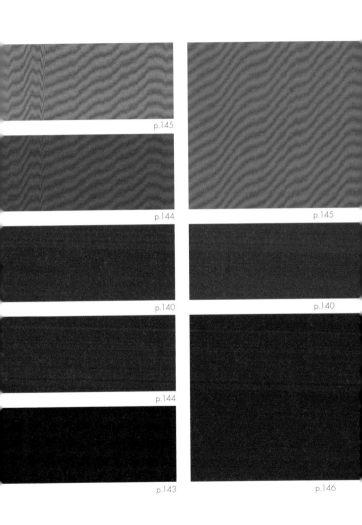

p.145

p.145

p.144

p.140

p.140

p.144

p.143

p.146

PINK Wild Rose to Raspberry

p.157

p.153

p.152

p.150

p.151

p.157

p.156

p.157

p.163

p.167

p.166

p.149

p.163

p.167

p.167

p.171

PURPLE Violet to Fig

p.183

p.177

p.181

p.177

p.178

p.181

p.178

p.177

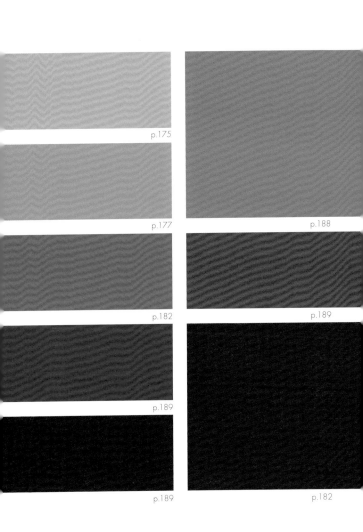

p.175

p.177

p.182

p.188

p.189

p.189

p.189

p.182

GREY Smoke to Charcoal

p.197

p.200

p.204

p.200

p.204

p.194

p.194

p.194

p.196

p.196

p.204

p.193

p.199

p.205

p.211

p.208

NATURAL String to Chocolate

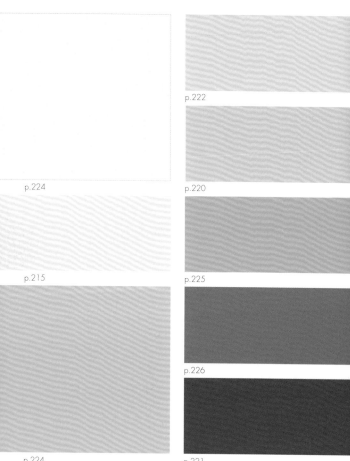

p.224

p.222

p.215

p.220

p.225

p.224

p.226

p.221

p.216

p.222

p.221

p.225

p.220

p.222

p.227

p.226

WHITE Paper to Snow